Ralph Maddern

Walk in the romantic vale of FFESTINIOG

PORTHMADOG

CRICIETH

to Sam Joe Robert

Focus Publications Ltd

First published in Great Britain 1986
Revised and re-published 1994

Focus Publications Ltd
9 Priors Road
Windsor
Berkshire SL4 4PD

ISBN: 1–872050–04–2

Printed in Great Brit[illegible]
Eyre & Spottiswo[illegible]

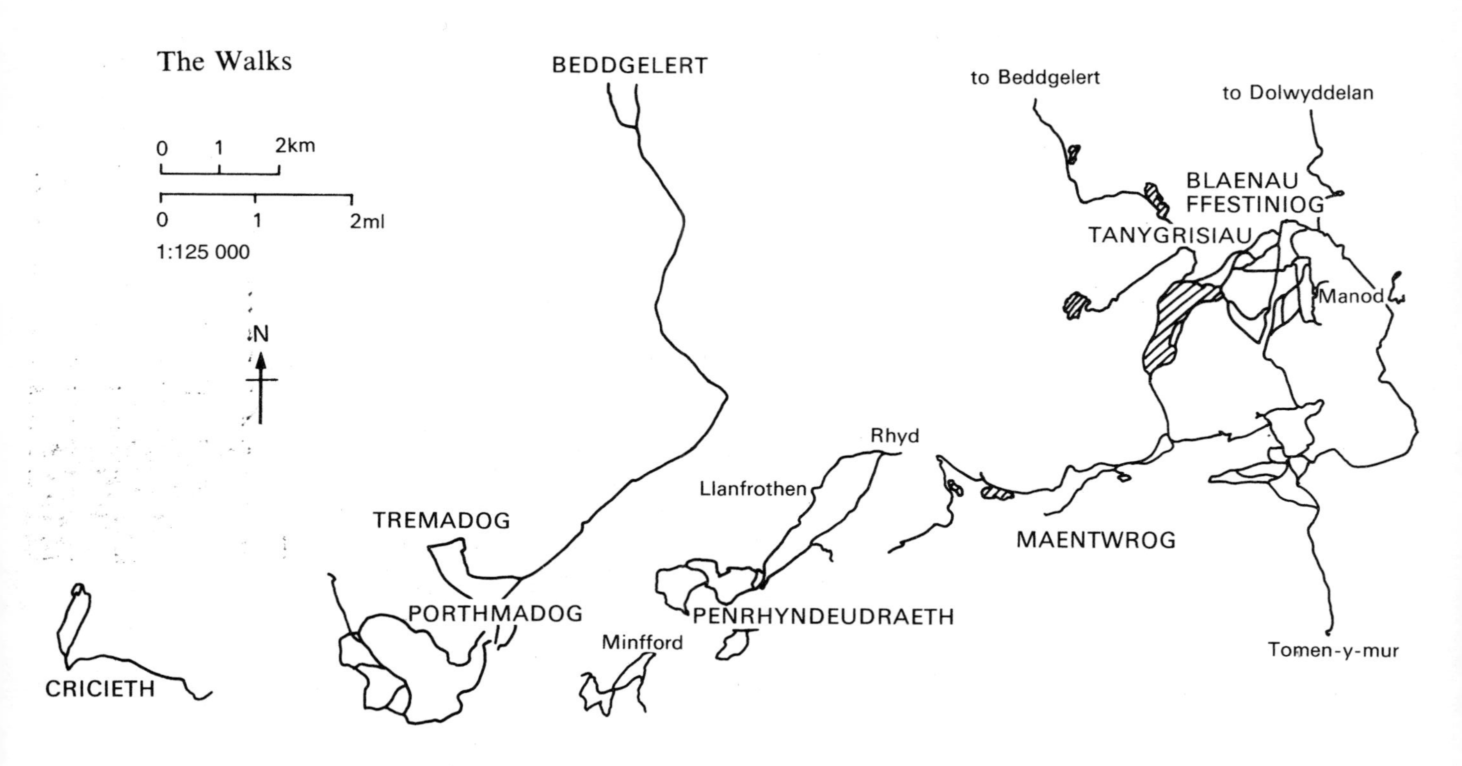
The Walks
0
1
2km
0
1
2ml
1:125 000
N
BEDDGELERT
to Beddgelert
to Dolwyddelan
BLAENAU
FFESTINIOG
TANYGRISIAU
Manod
Rhyd
Llanfrothen
TREMADOG
MAENTWROG
PORTHMADOG
PENRHYNDEUDRAETH
Minfford
Tomen-y-mur
CRICIETH

Contents

Illustrations

Outline Portraits

Compass Bearings

Pedometer Readings

and the romantic vale

Accuracy of position and direction is ensured by combining two kinds of measurement: distance registered by a pedometer, and direction recorded by a compass.

A pedometer reading may be taken to be correct to the nearest one-tenth of a kilometre or one hundred metres: 1.7km is within the range 1.65km to 1.75km, 1650 metres to 1750 metres.

A compass bearing of 080° can be accepted as lying within the arc 075° to 085°.

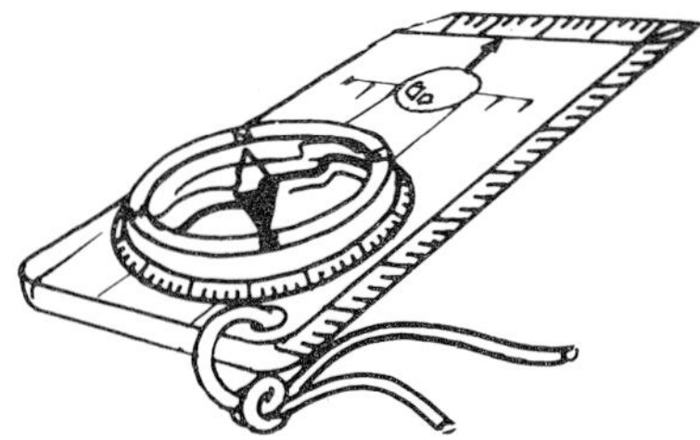

To determine a bearing, hold a hand compass in a horizontal position and allow the needle to steady. Turn the circle graduated in degrees until the N/S marking – 0°/360° to 180° – lies exactly beneath the needle.

If a bearing in this text is to be followed move the base platform until its centre line registers the required reading on the graduated circle.

If the bearing of an object from a position on the ground is required, move the base platform until its centreline is aligned with the object. Read the object's bearing on the graduated circle.

If seeking a bearing from an Ordnance Survey map in order to follow a direction on the ground,

★ place the centre of the graduated circle on the map position from which the bearing is to be taken
★ move the grid lines of the graduated circle to coincide with those of the OS map
★ align the base platforms centreline on the map with the object whose bearing is required and read the bearing on the graduated circle.

Welsh

Place names in Wales are fascinating because of the descriptions they offer of their locations. That is why interpretations are given where this is possible. Understanding what the name means is often a major clue to knowing the place itself. Pronunciation can be quite difficult for a non-Welsh speaker but it is worth trying to get the right sound. The main sounds, where these differ from English, are set out below.

a	as in *are*
c	always hard as in *car*
Ch	as in the Scottish *loch*
e	`ay' as in *say*
f	as in the English '*v*'
Ff	as in the English '*f*'
g	always hard as in *give*
Ll	place the tongue to form 'l' but emit a passage of air through the tongue to merge with the following letter
r	rolled more strongly than in English
Rh	both the 'r' and the 'h' are pronounced
Th	as in *both*
Dd	also `th' but as in *this*
u	'i' as in *it* or 'ee' as in *feet*
w	'oo' as in roost (Llanrwst = Llanroost) – it also works like the English 'w'
y	'u' as in *fun* or 'ee' as in *feet* or 'i' as in *pin* (you have to listen)

J, K, Q, V, X and Z do not appear in Welsh as these sounds are conveyed by other letters or diphthongs.

As with some Welsh poetry the evocative quality in the term *critch-cratch* eludes adequate representation in English. *Critch-cratch* refers to a gate hung in a U or V-shaped enclosure and is, therefore, impassable to stock animals. It is sometimes known as a 'kissing gate'.

Critch-cratch seems much more illustrative and evocative.

BLAENAU FFESTINIOG . . .
and its *wondrous sensations!*

To experience them one should launch out at the head of the Vale where trickling streams coalesce into gushing rivulets converging to form silky waterfalls of virgin purity yet untainted by the world downstream. In Blaenau the secret is to make for a height: any one will do for a beginning. Some heights are within the town; others are part of the grand sculpture of magnificent mountainous landscape.

If the sky is disgorging a flood, if a steam locomotive adds its smoke to plumes from coal fires, then we are fortunate in having an opportunity to imbibe an atmosphere representing the traditional Blaenau when men trudged to work on wet winter mornings, and back home in the evenings after spending the day at a quarry face. The product they produced satisfied a commercial need when Britain's towns were rapidly expanding. If that were the sole purpose of this place the community would have died when the market found it could satisfy demand for roofing slates with a cheaper, artificial product. Across the world are ghost towns that boomed then shrank to skeletons because nothing could sustain them when the source of their creation was exhausted.

No ghost stalks here. Here, industrialism was a catalyst: an agent that concentrated inherent cultural characteristics of the community it created. When the catalyst was withdrawn the community was shaken but something of enduring structure remained. Our purpose now is to discover its quality. To begin within the town itself.

Blaenau Ffestiniog late 19th century

Blaenau Ffestiniog: 3.2km, 2ml.

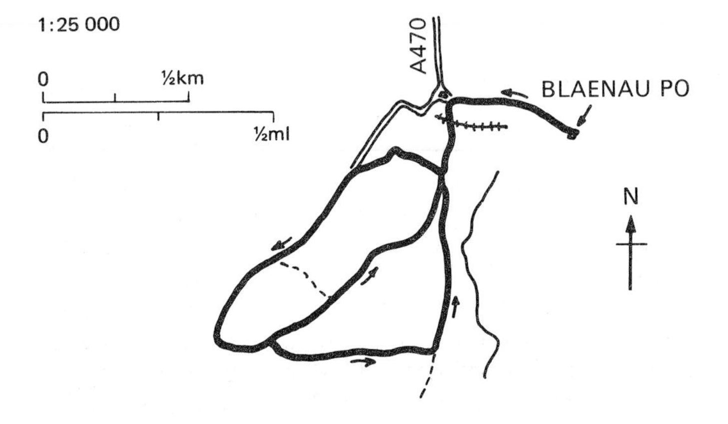

From the Blaenau PO (0.0km; elevation 244m, 800ft) walk NW along the A470 for 500m and turn left to the hump-backed bridge that spans the railway. If the steam train is on its way up the Vale this bridge offers an opportunity for an authentic taste of old Blaenau as the locomotive passes beneath to the station.

Continue past the square to the second turning right, along that street to the end, turn left then fork right along a tarmac path to the B4414 (1.1km), SW along the road for 300m, turn left onto a quarry road to a gate on the left (1.6km), bear NE and E to a gate and then a fence opening (2.0km). SE is a mound from which to view the valley and town.

If you are carrying a cassette recorder with head phones, or if your memory is sufficiently primed, this would be a place — standing above the town yet almost in it — to switch on *Côr Meibon y Brythoniaid*, or *Côr Meibion y Moelwyn*, or *The Royal Oakley Silver Band.* All have two essential qualities for continuity: high artistic standards attained through dedication, and a capacity for adapting to changing conditions.

The Royal Oakley Silver Band was formed in the mid-nineteenth century — as "the poor man's introduction to music" — by slate quarrymen who worked from seven in the morning until five in the afternoon. Now, half the band membership are teenagers who benefit from music tuition in schools. They offer a repertoire extending across a spectrum from marches through ballads to classical and modern popular composers. A century of folk memory has led the town to believe that its band will be a regular prize winner at competitions and eisteddfodau. Band membership may be different from times past but The Royal Oakley's attainments continue to match a long tradition of public expectation.

Côr Meibion y Moelwyn — The Moelwyn Male Voice Choir — is named after Y Moelwyn, that splendid massif standing guard on Blaenau's western frontier.

i. Oer ei drum, garw'i dremynt — yw erioed
A'i rug iddo'n emrynt;
Iach oror praidd a cherrynt
A'i greigiau'n organnau'r gwynt.

Cold its ridge, rugged its state — as always
Wrapped in heather cover;
Lush home of the flock and streams
And its rocks organs of the wind.

You can take your pick from among high quality performances in Latin, Italian, German, English and Welsh: Côr Meibion y Moelwyn has done it all as far from home as Iceland. However, this is not considered to be Côr Moelwyn's greatest accomplishment. That honour is bestowed upon a piece of the town's heritage — Rhiw Chapel — immaculately restored as the choir's headquarters where future performances are prepared, honed and polished, a process which visitors are welcome to observe.

At the 1985 National Eisteddfod in Rhyl, Côr Meibion y Moelwyn was awarded a first prize, as was Blaenau's other choir, Côr Meibion y Brythoniaid, a singular tribute to this cradle of choral excellence.

Y Brythoniaid refers to the Britons — The Celtic Britons and their language — a cherished tradition taken on international tours: to California; to countries on the Continent of Europe; to various towns in Britain; in appearances on television and radio. From stages of the wider world Y Brythoniaid returns to its twice-weekly rehearsals in Ysgol y Moelwyn, and to give concerts in local chapels and schools. Find one such concert, an entirely Welsh occasion, and you will have made a real discovery. Enjoy the unique treat, recall and savour it on this mound, or on any other height above Blaenau.

Walk 2

Blaenau Ffestiniog: 3.9km, 2½ml.

On reaching the B4414 (1.1km) from the Blaenau PO as in Walk 1, continue SW along the road for 700m, turn left — SE past the farm cottage *Tynddol* — the house in the meadow — to a fork (2.0km). The left fork (070°) leads to a gate (2.3km) and, as in Walk 1, rejoin the outward route.

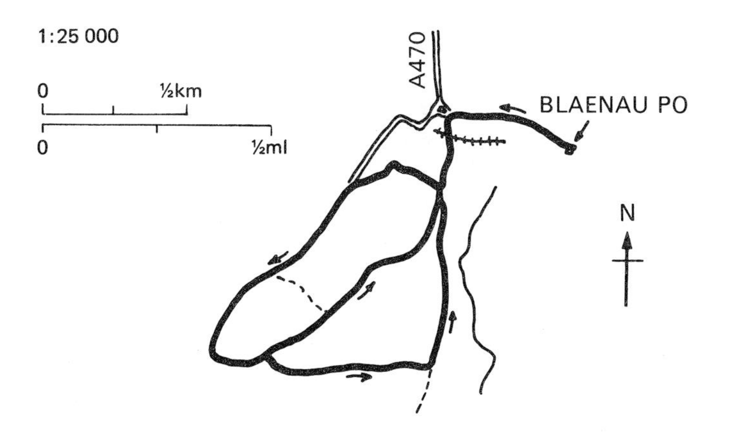

Walk 3

Blaenau Ffestiniog: 4.5km, 2.8ml.

Beyond the cottage Tynddol, as in Walk 2, take the right fork at 2.0km, bearing 150° right of the fence, veering to E beyond the field wall up onto a mound. Here is another point from which to view the valley and town. Descend the slope to the valley path (2.5km) and turn northward.

Walk 4

Blaenau — Cwmbowydd: 6km, $3\frac{3}{4}$ml.

As in Walk 1 continue along the B4414 (from 1.1km) to a critchcratch (2.7km), bear E and SE up and around the craggy outcrop known as *Pen-y-cefn* — top of the ridge. Veer NE down to the valley track that bears northward along the floor of the cwm to the town.

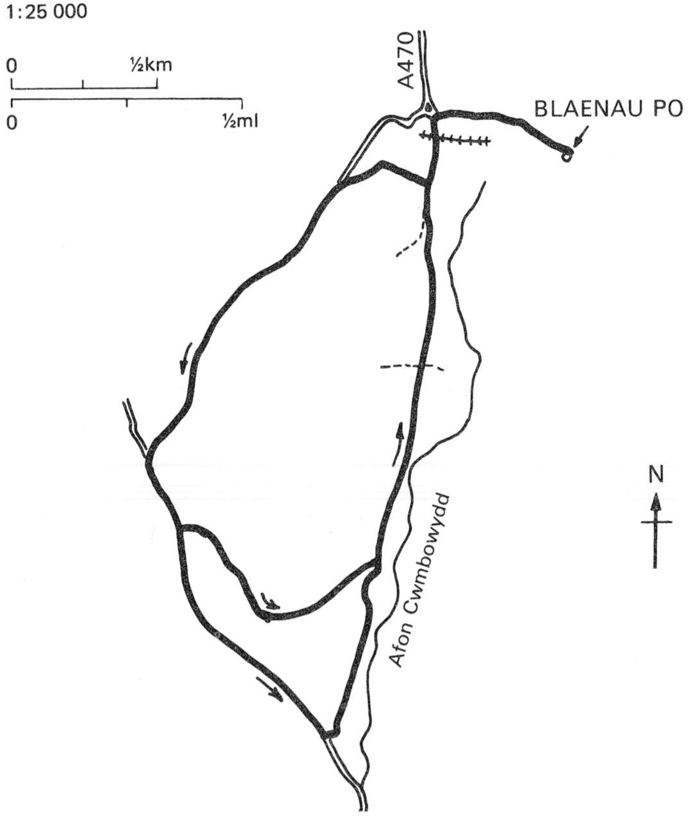

Walk 5

Blaenau — Cwmbowydd: 6.5km, 4.1ml.

This route includes the entire length of Cwmbowydd. Follow the B4414 from 1.1km to 3.5km, turn left (E) then northward into the wide valley sheltering within its rugged horizon of ridges.

ii. Wele rith fel ymyl rhod — o'n cwmpas,
Campwaith dewin hynod;
Hen linell bell nad yw'n bod,
Hen derfyn nad yw'n darfod.

Behold a guise like an orbit edge — surrounding,
Masterpiece of a remarkable magician;
An old distant line that is not in being,
An old boundary that does not end.

A couple of centuries ago this path along the floor of the cwm was a traditional packhorse trail used by drovers taking herds of animals off to England. Now, it is straddled by Blaenau's re-located sewage works, a feature which one can scarcely fail to appreciate even at a distance.

Skirt left round the works and on to a wall gate (4.6km). There is a path intersection at 4.8km (see Walk 6); 200m further on fork right and descend NE to a footbridge (5.1km) spanning a confluence of the Afon Bowydd with a tributary. Up through the woods to the massive rock supporting Blaenau's secondary school (5.4km) and into the town.

Blaenau — Cwmbowydd: 1.4km, 0.9ml.

From Blaenau PO (0.0km), turn left (SW) down the adjacent street over the railway and follow the road right, then left, SW past the school into the woods, south and southeastward to a stile (0.9km) by the Cwmbowydd Farm drive. Turn right (SW) along the farm drive, fork left beyond the gate into the field (1.1km), cross the footbridge SW of the house, continue SW past the barn and W over the wall to join the valley path.

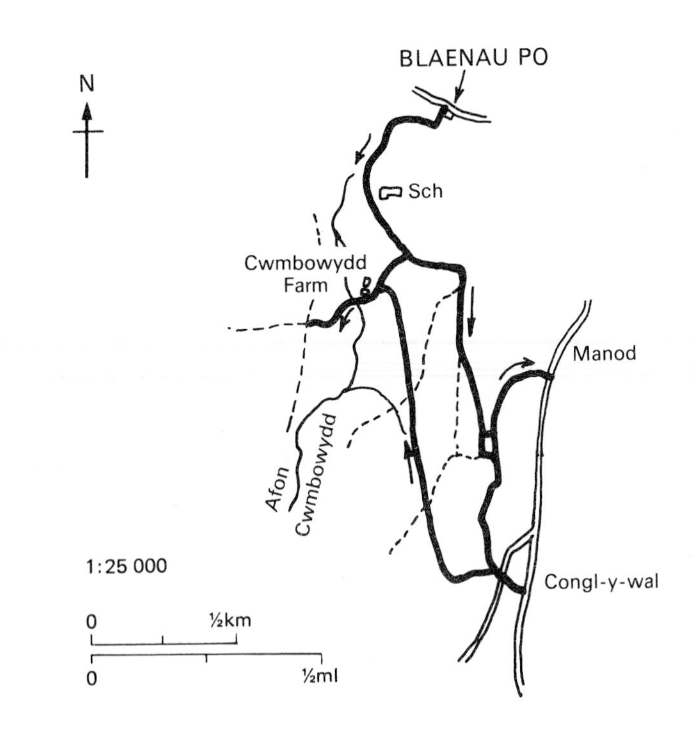

Walk 7

Blaenau — Manod: 2.4km, 1½ml.

As for Walk 6 to the stile by the Cwmbowydd Farm drive (0.9km), turn E along the drive then S (1.1km), take the left fork southward beyond a critch-cratch (1.4km), veer left and continue alongside the railway. Cross the bridge, left (1.9km), and follow the field path to Manod Village, lying at the foot of Manod-bach. (Refer to Walk 10).

Walk 8

Blaenau — Congl-y-wal — Blaenau: 4.9km, 3.1ml.

From the bridge over the railway (1.9km in Walk 7), continue southward to the next bridge (2.0km), turn right and follow the path on 200°, then SE to a stile (2.4km) opposite Congl-y-wal. *Congl* means corner. *Congl-y-wal*: corner of the wall.

If returning to Blaenau, turn right (W), continue past a barn, then northward to a stile (2.8km) and, 100m further on, converge with a path on the left.

Taking the right fork the outward path may be rejoined (3.2km).

Taking the left fork at 2.9km, continue northward through Cwmbowydd Farm to a footbridge (3.9km), through a gated opening to the stile by the farm drive (4.0km), and northward through the woods past the school (4.4km) to the town.

Crew of Oakley Quarry c1900

Graigddu quarrymen returning home down trolley track

Rockmen's workplace

Splitting, sawing and dressing slates

Blaenau — the Quarries and northward: 2.7km, 1.7ml.

From Blaenau PO walk E/SE along the A470 for almost 200m, take the third turning left and continue N, following the quarry road as it curves eastward between hills of slate debris. At 1.0km, turn left across the route of an old tramway and follow the road NW. Before reaching a quarry building about 500m further on, turn right and maintain a north bearing beyond the quarry workings to a gate and stile at the base of Ffridd-y-bwlch (2.4km). Continue uphill on a bearing of 350°, skirting the corner of a fence, to the left summit (2.7km). Here is a point to see the quarries arranged as a giant artist's model.

The creators were men working in groups of four: two rockmen who extracted the rock and two men who dressed the rough blocks and split them into usable slates. These groups were dependent upon many others such as surveyors, miners, hauliers, platelayers and machinery attendants. Such a pattern of interdependence is a familiar feature of many mining communities but here in Wales there was a distinct cultural aspect. This can be illustrated by imagining a group of quarry workers taking their midday meal.

A sealed-off section of tunnel converted into *y caban*. Under a *Llywydd*, a chairman, a wide-ranging discussion: on Monday and Tuesday the debate might be about sermons preached in the chapels on Sunday. A good Llywydd sought to have members of his *caban* probe depths of meanings. For the remainder of the week the *caban* might turn to recitation, poetry, choral activities, performances of brass bands. The *caban* also served as a forum for political discussion, and as a cell for organising the North Wales Quarrymen's Union whose stormy history is part of Britain's trade union story.

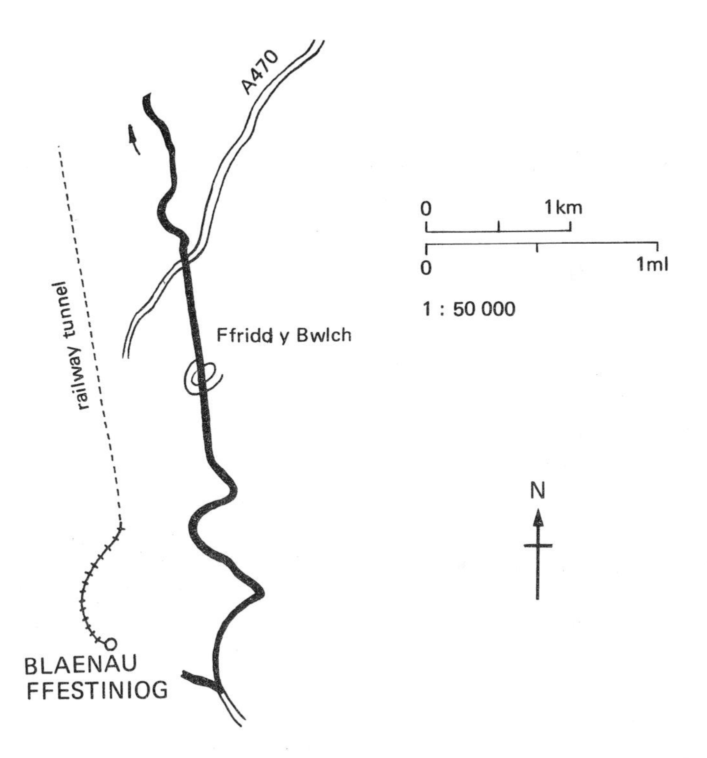

The route northward bears 350° down to the A470 (3.6km, 2.2ml), across the road and along wheeltracks passing Moel Dyrnogydd on the left and on to Dolwyddelan (14.5km, 9.1ml) as described in **Walk in Magnificent Snowdonia**.

iii. Bachgen dengmlwydd gerddodd ryw ben bore,
Lawer dydd yn ôl, i gwr y gwaith;
Gobaith fflachiai yn ei lygaid gleision
Olau dengmlwydd i'r dyfodol maith.

Cryf oedd calon hen y glas glogwyni,
Cryfach oedd ei ebill ef a'i ddur;
Chwyddodd gyfoeth gŵr yr aur a'r faenol
O'i enillion prin a'i amal gur.

Neithiwr daeth tri gŵr o'r gwaith yn gynnar;
Soniwyd am y graig yn torri'n ddwy;
Dygwyd rhywun tua'r tŷ ar elor,
Segur fydd cŷn a'r morthwyl mwy.

A ten year old boy walked early one morn,
Many a day ago, to begin work;
Hope flashed in his blue eyes
The light of ten years to the vast future.

Strong was the old heart of the blue crags,
Stronger was his gimlet and steel;
Wealth of the man of gold and manor swelled
From his meagre earnings and frequent pain.

Last night came three men from the works early,
Their story was of rock breaking in two;
Someone was brought to the house on a bier,
Idle will be chisel and hammer from now.

Walk 10

Blaenau — Manod-bach summit: 1.9km, 1.2ml.

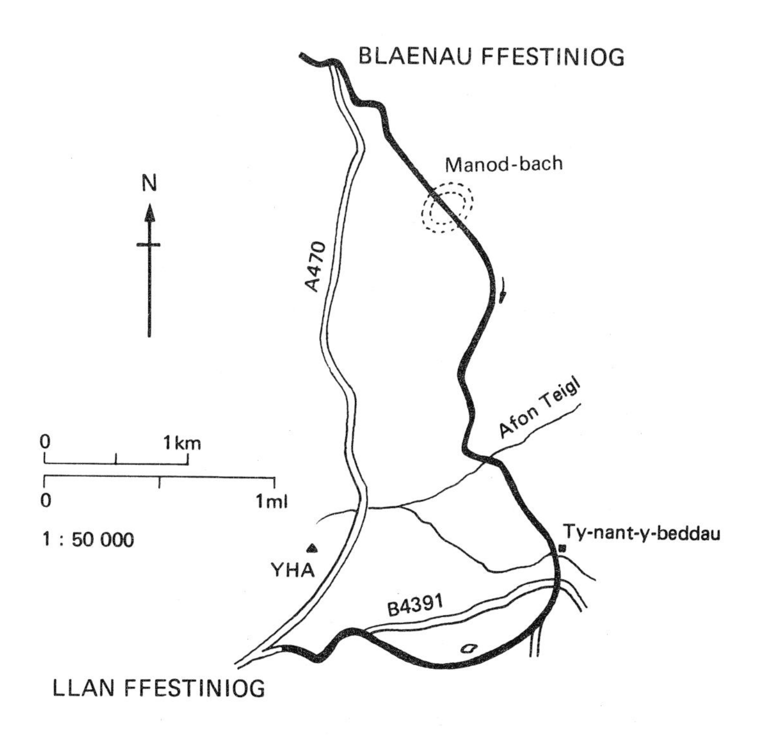

From the Blaenau PO walk E/SE along the A470 for 300m, fork left at the fifth turning left and continue round the massive boulder formation onto a path that winds up to a lane (0.4km). Turn right, follow the lane, bearing 150°, to a path (0.5km) and on to a T-junction opposite a row of terraced cottages (0.8km). Turn right and continue to the site of an old woollen mill (1.0km).

Stand on the little stone bridge awhile. If Blaenau's weather has been living up to its reputation feel the massive power which this mill used to harness, tumbling down from Manod-bach that rocky mass looming skywards.

Turn left along the path by the bridge and begin the climb. Mark a point with the eye on the summit ridge, general bearing 140°, and continue across the old tramway track to the summit (elevation 473m, 1550ft).

A splendid viewpoint. To the east is the larger Manod-mawr, and between the two is Llyn y Manod, the Manod lake, a peaceful retreat for anglers. To the south-west is Llan Ffestiniog and, facing us across the valley to the west, the Moelwyns, those two solid sentinels which a bard once transformed.

iv. Gwnaeth Duw'r ddau Foelwyn, meddant i mi,
O garreg nad oes ei chadarnach hi.

Ond wrth syllu arnynt ambell awr
Ar fore o wanwyn, amheuaf yn fawr.

Mai o bapur sidan y torrodd o
Y ddau ohonynt ymhell cyn co',

A'u pastio'n sownd ar yr wybren glir
Rhag i'r awel eu chwythu ar draws y tir.

God made both Moelwyns, I am told,
From the strongest stone.

But gazing at them through a carefree hour
On a spring morning, I doubt it greatly.

From silk paper he cut both
Long before memory,

And pasted them securely on the clear sky
So the breeze does not blow them across the land.

Finished slates ready for transport

If we are not returning to Blaenau our attention must turn southward to Llan, the original Ffestiniog, a retreat in the heart of the heartland, a sanctuary for the embattled rebel.

Walk 11

Manod-bach summit — Llan Ffestiniog: 6.1km, 3.8ml.

Descend on 140°, cross a stream and join a path from Llyn y Manod at a wall gate. Continue alongside a wall and through an opening 150m further on to a pair of ruins, Bryn-eithin. About 50m beyond the ruins turn left (160°), follow a path across fields to wheeltracks, turn right (220°) and continue down past the farmhouse, Teiliau-mawr (2.1km). Veer left (SE) from the farmyard, past the house Minafon on the left, across the Afon Teigl to a stile and up the hill to a wall stile. Continue SE, crossing the Afon Nant Llyn-morwynion and passing the farmhouse, Ty-nant-y-beddau, on the left. This is a land of streams!

v. Ffrydiau mân llethrau'r Manod — yn bwrlwm
I gafn Barlwyd isod;
Lli' ar rus unlliw yr ôd,
Êl yn dawel ar dywod.

Small streams from the slopes of Manod — bubbling
To the trough of Marlwyd below;
The flow starts the colour of snow,
Goes quietly on sand.

Continue up hill, across the B4391 to a stile and on, bearing 200°, to a farm road (3.5km). Veer right and follow the road for 200m to a gate on the right where the wheeltracks bear 230°. After passing a small reservoir on the right veer to W and continue to a gated wall opening and wall steps (4.8km). Cross the field (300°) to a barn, follow wheeltracks to a critch-cratch and turn left along the B4391 to Llan Ffestiniog PO.

Walk 12

Valley route to Llan Ffestiniog: 6.4km, 4ml.

Follow the route from Blaenau PO described in Walks 6 and 7 to the stile by the Cwmbowydd Farm drive (0.9km). Continue E along the drive for 200m, turn right (S) and take the right fork (SW) via the town's rubbish dump to a gate and stile (1.7km), veer S to SW through woodland up and around the *bryn* (hill), down to the river and along the east side of Afon Cwmbowydd to a stile near the bridge carrying the B44l4 (3.3km).

Alternatively — if, for example, the river is running high — veer south from the bryn to a path junction, then SW past the house *Tan-y-bryn* — under the bryn — and southward to the stile near the bridge carrying the B4414 (3.3km).

Turn left to a critch-cratch 50m along the service road, SE and E up the hill to a wall stile (3.7km), down the hill to the A496 (3.9km), across the field to the farm road (4.0km) and on through three gated openings to a farm drive (4.1km).

Llan Ffestiniog may now be seen beyond the farther bryn (160°). Continue past Pengwern Old Hall Farm on the right to a stile on the north side of the Afon Dwyryd (4.7km), turn left (E) to two stiles and waterfalls. Lucky is the walker who sees these falls in full flood — with creaming foam draping ancient boulders, creating little rainbows if the sun should be shining between the leaves.

Then there is an old mill.

vi. Gweld y melinydd uniaith, ffraeth ei eiriau
Yn gwynnu yng nghynefin dawch ei hynt.
Canai wrth ollwng grawn yr haidd a'r gwenith
I'r gwancus gafn, gan borthi'r meini mâl,
A'r henfro'n disgwyl am sacheidiau'r fendith
Tra sychai yntau'r chwŷs o'i lychlyd dâl.

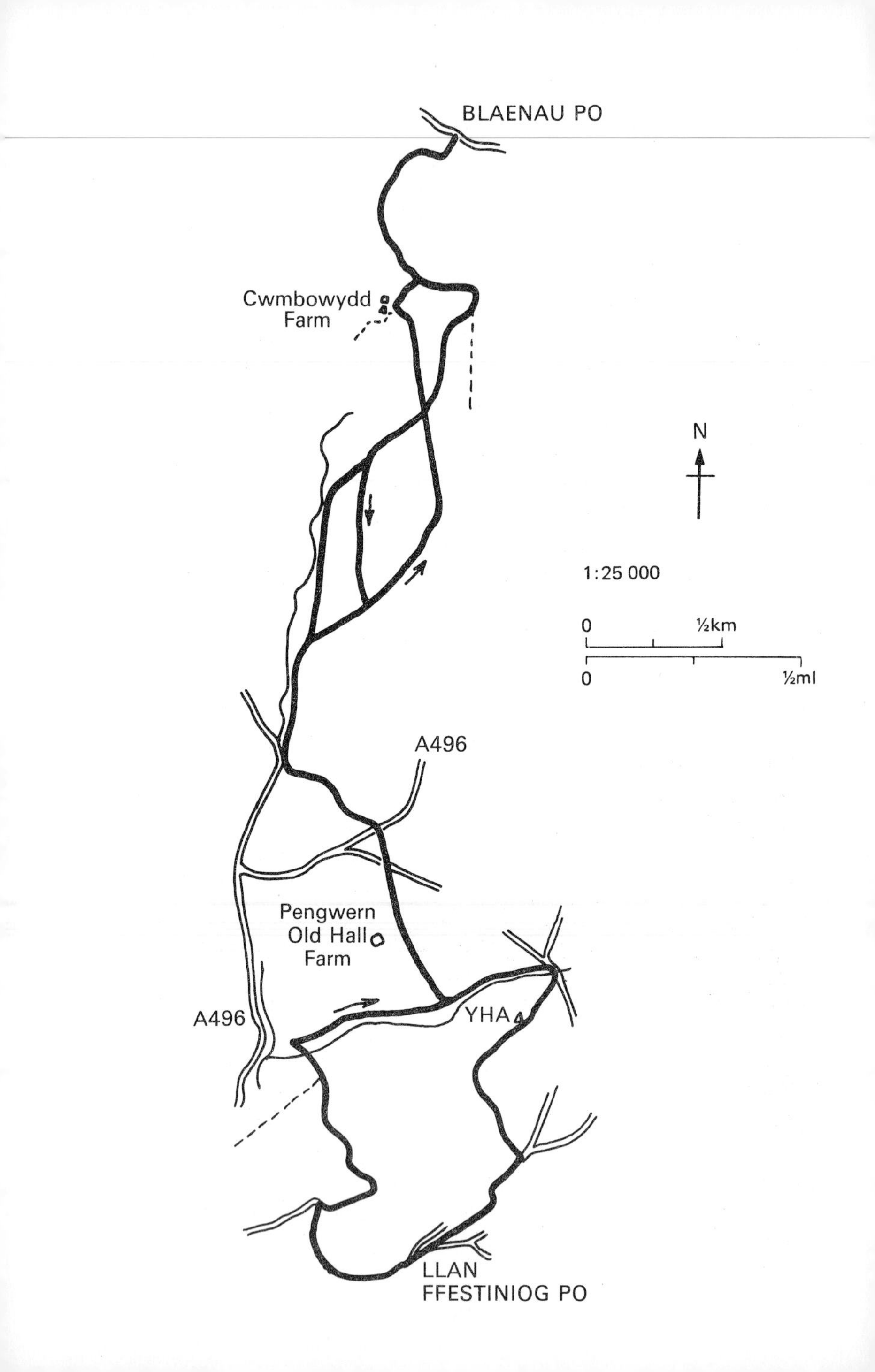
BLAENAU PO
Cwmbowydd
Farm
N
1:25 000
0
½km
0
½ml
A496
Pengwern
Old Hall
Farm
A496
YHA
LLAN
FFESTINIOG PO

The monoglot miller, witty in language
Whitening in his hazy environment.
He sings while feeding grains of barley and wheat
Into the trough and between the grinding stones,
And the district waiting for sacks of blessing
As he wipes sweat from his dusty forehead.

Turn right and right again over the bridge that spans the river, follow the track S/SW to the Youth Hostel (5.4km), SW and SE past Blaen-ddol to the A470, cross the road and continue up to the Llan Ffestiniog PO.

Ffestiniog

Retreat
Sanctuary
Self-sufficiency

Penffestin is a mail cap or helmet. *Ffestinio* suggests a need to hurry. Whether one should hurry past this place or to it, avoid it or gain protection from its terrain and climate, may depend upon the point of view. Certainly, invaders have hurried past it: the Yorkists and Lancastrians in 1468 and the Royalists and Roundheads almost two centuries later. For others it offered a safe embrace where an identity could be lost and another found. Here was a world apart: external relations were in the hands of a storekeeper who drove a packhorse to Wrexham twice a year to pick up some oddments that locals could not produce. His return was a landmark in the calendar celebrated at the Pengwern Arms, known then — in the eighteenth century — as *Yr Efail* — the smithy — because it was kept by a blacksmith. Here, one could live within a world in itself: isolated, self-sufficient and, of necessity, self-reliant. Now, it is necessary to depart from the village — immerse oneself amongst the forests, fields, streams — to imbibe the sense of how it felt to be here.

Walk 13

Llan to Blaenau: 7.5km, 4.7ml.

From Llan Ffestiniog PO (0.0km; elevation: 183m, 600ft) walk W along the B4391 past the Pengwern Arms to a gate on the right (0.8km), eastward to a critch-cratch (1.0km) then northward through gates (1.1, 1.3, 1.6km) down through woods to a path junction (1.7km). (The path on the left continues south-westward for 800m to the A496 where another path leads to Dduallt: see Walk 18). Northward 150m is a footbridge over the Afon Dwyryd, and 150m further on is a footbridge over a tributary, from which paths westward reach the A496 in about 100m. From the south side of the second footbridge ascend N then eastward onto a ridge that divides two valleys and introduces a romantic world of deciduous woodland secreting waterfalls dressed in frilly white foam.

Rejoin the outward path (2.8km), turn left and continue NW. On reaching the stile near the bridge carrying the B4414 (4.3km, 2.7ml), turn northward up the farm drive, veer to the right before reaching the house and continue NE and E up the path to stiles at 4.9km and 5.2km. Further along at the path junction (5.4km), veer northward to Cwmbowydd Farm and the stile at the side of the farm drive (6.6km), up through the woods and into the town.

Walk 14

Llan - Rhaeadr Cynfal (Cynfal Falls): 1.3km, 0.8ml.

From Llan PO follow the B4391 SW past the Pengwern Arms for 200m, turn left (150°) to a stile, gate and foot-bridge (0.5km), a critch-cratch, a wall stile (0.6km), then bear 200° veering to SE and a gate at 1.1km.

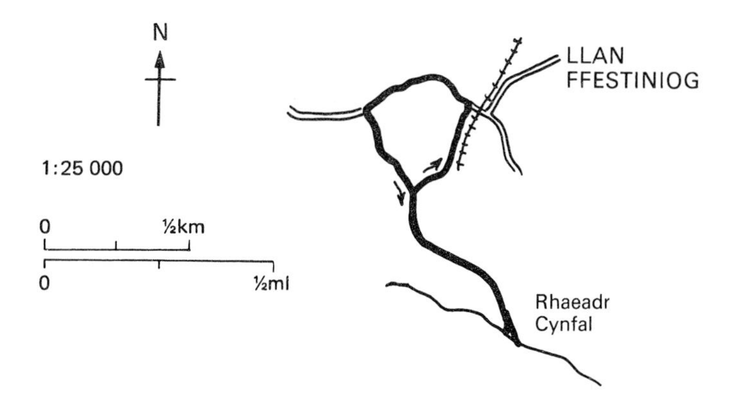

Fork right to the sound of flowing water crashing into primeval caverns. The river squeezes through a narrow opening into a three-sided chamber, then down through a narrower opening into a smaller *ystafell* where it seems to disappear beneath massive boulders. Only after climbing up the stone steps does one catch a view of it flowing tranquilly on its way down the Vale.

Taking the left fork at the gate (1.1km), continue down the path 200m to a footbridge. No frothy white gems here. The long view upstream — especially if Ffestiniog favours us with one of its grey skies — reveals a spectrum of colour from deep black through a range of browns to amber and fluffy fawn.

If returning to Ffestiniog, the town may be entered at its south-eastern end near the railway bridge.

Walk 15

Rhaeadr Cynfal — Tomen-y-mur: 4.4km, 2¾ml.

Leave the falls and enter a different historical age — back in time nearly 2000 years. From the footbridge (0.0km) walk S and SW to stiles at 1.5km, 1.7km and on to the drive of Cynfal-fawr. Veer left to a stile (1.8km) NE of the farmhouse.

Continue under the railway bridge (1.9km) and southward to two stiles on either side of the A470 (2.2km). South on 160° and a stile over a slate fence (2.9km), 150° to the next stile (3.0km) and continue S alongside the slate fence to a farm drive (3.4km), then to a tarmac road and the site of the Roman amphitheatre at Tomen-y-mur.

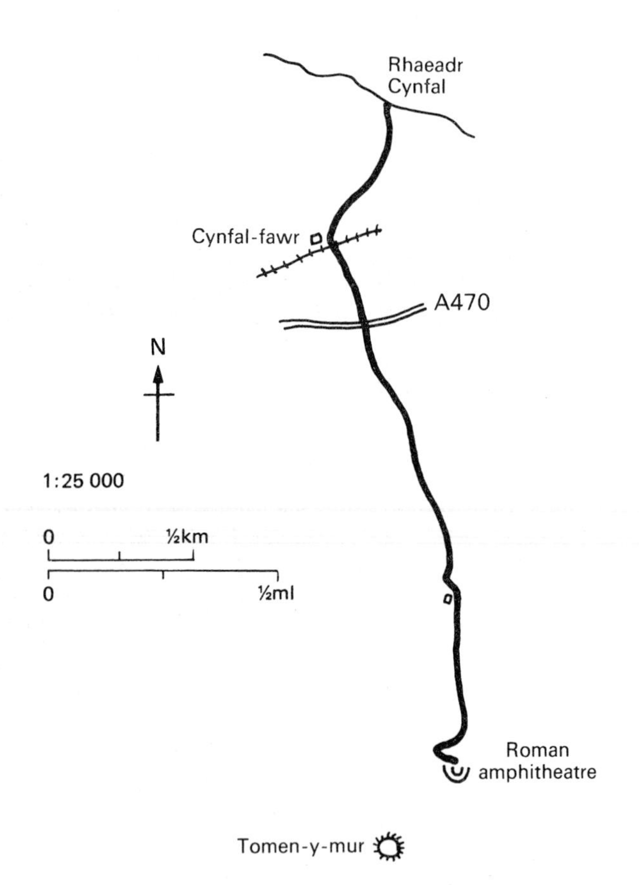

Cynfal Bridge, Ffestiniog 1907

Tomen-y-mur

Pivotal Fort in Roman Britain

If it were not for the unusual mound, 400m to the SW, one would pass it by as a dip in the ground like any other on the surface of Wales. That 30ft-high mound, or motte, raised by William Rufus — King William II — may have become the site of a castle but for the intervention of Gruffydd ap Cynan (1055–1137), ruling prince of Gwynedd, who drove William back to Chester in the winter of 1095, thereby securing for Wales almost two centuries of independence. Gruffydd was a guerrilla fighter who used tactics of ambush, dispersion, concentration, surprise — in conditions of a Welsh winter with masterly effect. William was a strategist who sought to complete England's conquest of the British land mass, eliminating a menacing threat to his flank. He was less successful than the Romans who, a thousand years earlier, easily over-ran north Wales and immediately recognised the strategic advantages of this location. The fort established here on a four-acre site following Agricola's conquest about 78 AD, formed the southern corner of a network encompassing Snowdonia. The pivotal aspect of the fort may be appreciated by noting its radiating lines of communication : roads north-westward to Segontium (Caernarfon), northward to Caer Llugwy and Caerhun, south-eastward to Caer Gai at the SW end of Bala Lake, southward to Moridunum (Carmarthen). Tomen-y-mur was probably a training base for the entire region, as the camps at Dolddinas, 2.4km SE, would suggest — at least until about the year 120 when Roman power had been consolidated and the strategic thrust was northward for the building of Hadrian's Wall. As part of a training complex the amphitheatre would have been used for demonstrating combat techniques.

The return trek north is worth making for its magnificent views. A full circle of ridges and summits displaying a medley of blues, greens, browns; contrasted, possibly, by a drape of mist veiling Eryri's rugged faces, with Llan and Blaenau arranged as tiny models on the landscape.

Walk 16

Rhaeadr Cynfal — Ceunant Cynfal (Cynfal Gorge) —
Llan Ffestiniog : 2.1km, 1.3ml.

From the footbridge (0.0km) bear westward above the south bank along a pleasant path with stiles at 0.3km and 0.8km. Continue on 330° for 450m and turn right, down to a footbridge (1.3km) which is in deep seclusion of the ceunant, and into quietude embraced by the sound of the river.

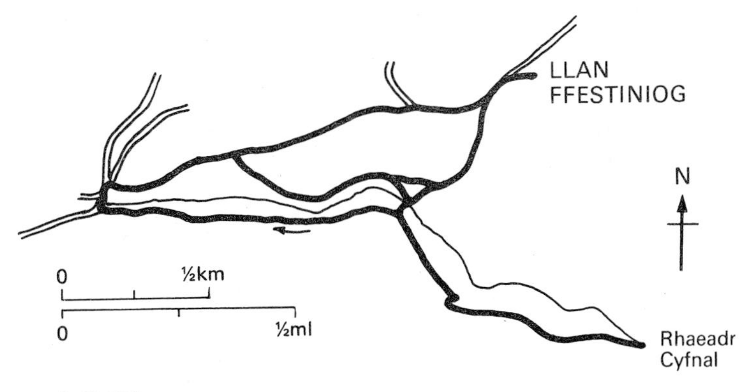

Timelessness is here at the bottom of the gorge, a sense of what was, what is, what will be.

vii. 'Tyn ariant geunant, ar daith i'r gweunydd,
Ei rwydi grisial o'r gwridog rosydd:
Dirwyn ei foliant i'r cadarn foelydd,
A'i sain bereiddia holl swyn boreddydd.

The silver gorge draws, on a journey to meadow,
Its crystal nets from blushing creeked moors:
Its songs twist to indomitable hills,
And its sound sweetens all the day's magic.

Climb up the bank E to a stile (1.4km) and then to a gate (1.5km). Veer NE to a stile (1.7km), along the edge of the field to a gate by the roadside (1.9km) and turn right to the Llan PO.

Walk 17

Llan Ffestiniog — Ceunant Cynfal south and north:
3.7km, 2.3ml.

From Llan PO (0.0km) bear westward past the Pengwern Arms to a gate (0.2km), descend along the edge of the field (S/SW) to a stile (0.4km), SW to a gate (0.6km); descend on 240° to a stile (0.8km) and down to the footbridge. Up the south bank join the path lying E/W (0.9km), turn right (W) and enjoy the pleasant woodland with whatever thoughts that might bring.

viii.
Haul gwyn ac anadl gwanwyn yn ddistaw a ddaw i ddwyn
Dyli drwy bob gwythïen, hudo o'r pridd waed i'r pren;
Annog rhuddin i'w gwreiddiau, a phuraf fêr i'w ffyrlhau,
Gwynt a haul, hwy gânt o hud siglo eu crud mwsoglyd.

White sun and breath of spring quietly will come to bring
A flux through every vein, drawing from earth blood to wood;
Enticing through roots, purest marrow to its form,
Wind and sun, incessantly rocking moss-covered cradles.

At the main road (2.0km) turn right and, beyond the bridge, right again and follow the path above the northern bank to a wall opening on the left (2.6km).

To return directly to Llan veer left through the opening and continue to the B4391 (3.2km) and along to the PO. On the bryn — or if walking E to W — a glance westward takes in the length of the Vale extending seawards between its immaculately sculptured hills clothed in native deciduous, while round the half-circle northward are the summits and ridges of the Vale's head.

Alternatively, at the wall opening (2.6km) a fork right (SE) leads to another (3.3km), where the left fork trails 150m through a plantation to a gate. Bear NE to a stile (3.7km), along the edge of the field to a gate (3.9km) by the roadside (B4391) and on to the PO.

The right fork at 3.3km leads down to the footbridge at the bottom of the ceunant.

Walk 18

Llan Ffestiniog — Dduallt Railway Station: 4.7km, 3ml.

From the PO (0.0km) SW along the B4391 for 100m, turn right (NW) by the Pengwern Arms, follow the lane to its end and turn right to a gate (not the critch-cratch) on the left. Continue down the field to a gate on the right and turn left to a gate in the corner of the field (0.6km).

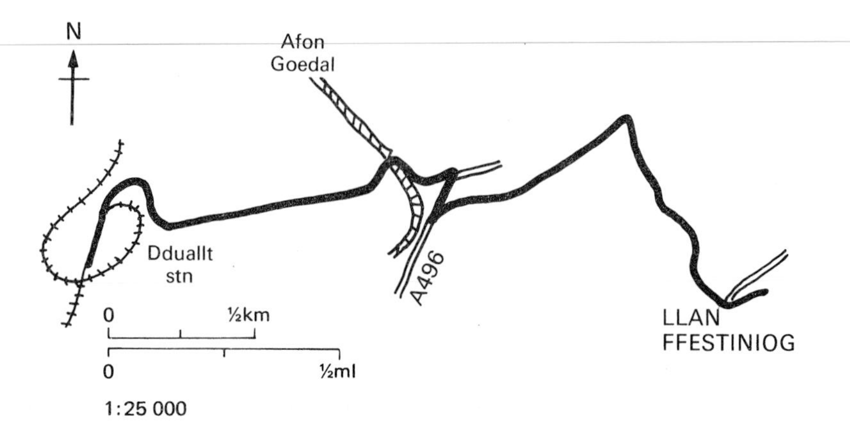

Bear 350° across the field to a gate (0.7km), continue to gates lower down passing a cottage on the left, NE then NW to a gate (1.0km) and turn right (N) to a barn and a path junction (1.1km). Turn left (250°) and continue westward through a gate (1.3km) to a farm driveway (1.8km) and on to the A496. Turn sharp right and, 150m along the road, left along a driveway to a path 100m further on into the Nature Reserve, Coed Cymerau, and upstream to a footbridge (2.6km) spanning the Afon Goedal. A path winds up through woodland to a plantation submerging ruggedly textured rocks, to a stile (3.3km) and two more stiles (3.6km). Up the hill there is the bed of the old Ffestiniog line about 30m from the new route.

Standing opposite the track one may chance to hear an energetic locomotive chugging just beyond the hillside, sounding its whistle to assure the world at large that it is alive and well. Down the track 400m is Dduallt station. The down train passes round the loop coming to rest opposite the up train which may then puff away to Tanygrisiau.

The Ffestiniog in 1907

Walk 19

Dduallt Station — Plas y Dduallt: 0.7km, $\frac{1}{2}$ml.

From the southern end of the platform (0.0km), cross the line, walk beneath the railway bridge, veer right (SW then W), enjoy a splendid view down the Vale, pass through a gate (0.5km) over the line and three stiles, to arrive at Plas y Dduallt — Dduallt Manor — delightfully situated in this secluded location with a reputation of once having provided a resting place for the leader of England's revolutionary parliamentary army, Oliver Cromwell, in hot pursuit of the King's men.

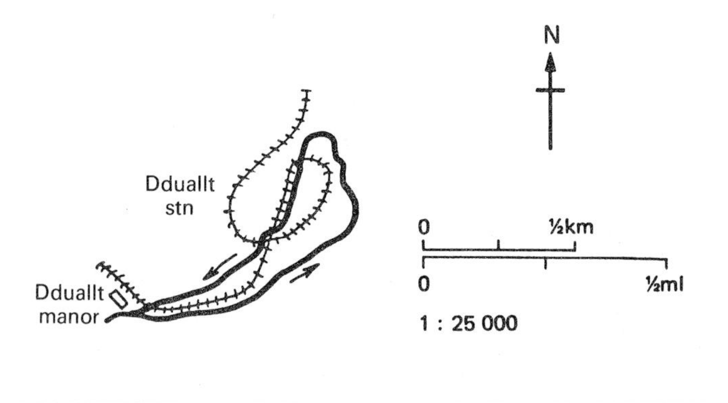

Walk 20

Plas y Dduallt — Dduallt Station: 1.6km, 1ml.

From the Manor (0.0km) walk SE and E to a gate (0.4km) and a wall (0.8km), NE and N through the woods arriving north of the loop to rejoin the route of Walk 18.

Walk 21

Dduallt Station — Blaenau: 7.7km, 4.8ml.

From the station (0.0km) follow the old railway track and the new, northward to the southern end of the reservoir (1.5km), forking right round the eastern shore to a wall stile (3.3km) opposite the power station, E to a footbridge and on to the B4414 (4.1km).

Turn right to a critch-cratch 200m along the road, E and SE up and around the bryn and NE down to the valley

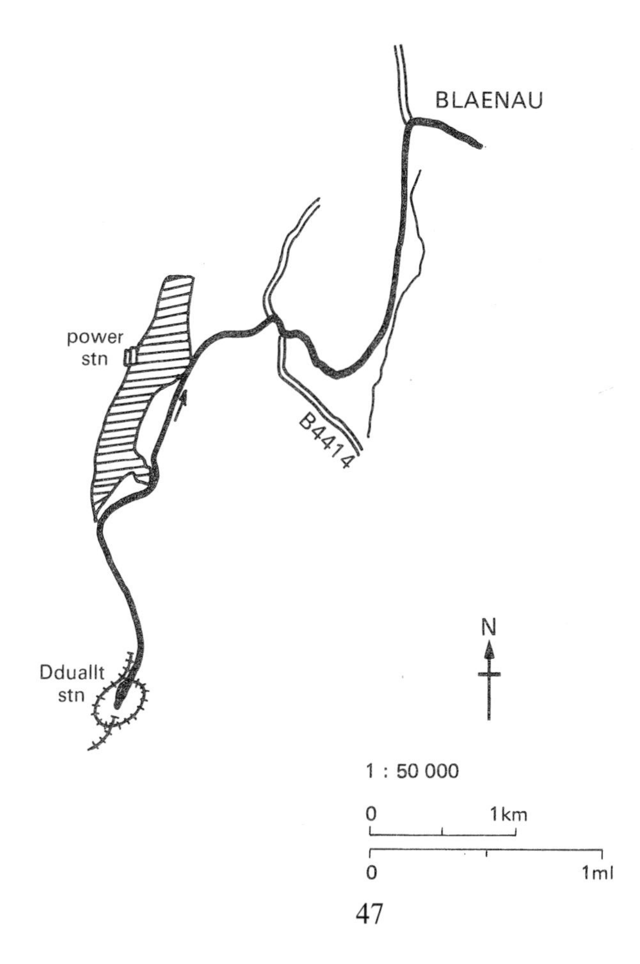

track. Follow the track northward along the floor of Cwm Bowydd, up through the woods and into the town.

Walk 22

Blaenau — Tanygrisiau Railway Station:
2.7km, 1.7ml.

As in Walk 1 to the B4414 and SW along the road to a stile on the right (1.4km). Beyond the next stile veer left (250°) and continue to a bridge over a stream, a headwater of the Afon Goedol — woodland river — which flows southward through the enchanting Coed Cymerau to join the Vale's main river, the Afon Dwyryd.

Turn left along the road, continue to the PO and W to the railway station.

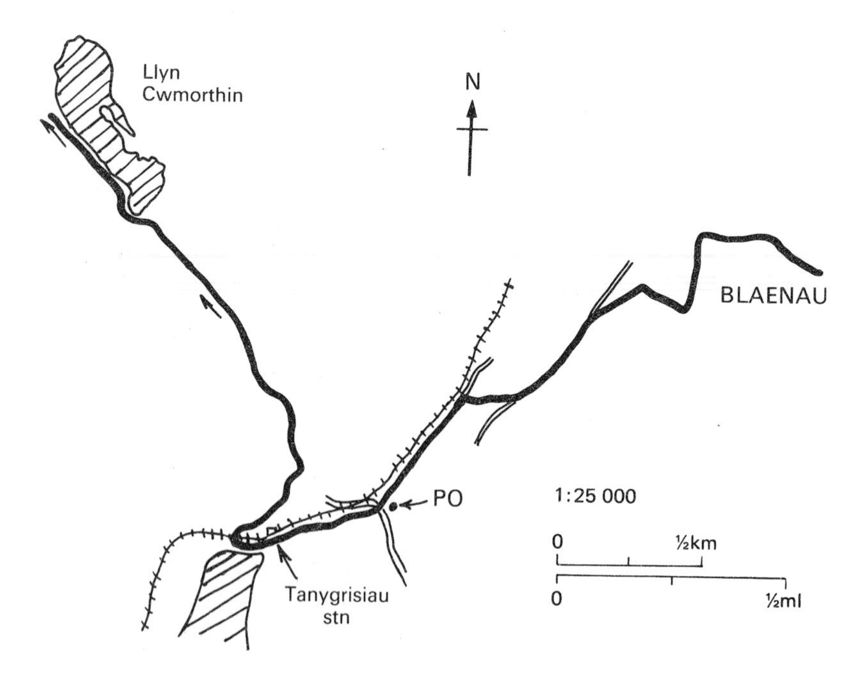

Walk 23

Tanygrisiau — Llyn Cwmorthin and westward:
1.5km, 0.9ml.

From the railway station (0.0km) bear W to a path near the Information Centre, northward to a village road, turn left, then NW along the old quarry track to the southern tip of Llyn Cwmorthin (1.3km). Fork left past the ruined chapel, veer W and SW up the slope to the site of disused quarry buildings. The route westward — see: **Walk in magnificent Snowdonia** — takes one past Llyn Cwmcorsiog and on to the enchanting Llyn yr Adar — lake of birds — elevation 2000ft, and down into the Nantgwynant Valley and Beddgelert (13.5km 8½ml) through fields where the rhododendron plant advances rampantly, excluding indigenous flora.

Tanygrisiau

Grisiau, meaning stairs, refers to the gradients of all routes westward. *Tanygrisiau:* under the stairs, which you, together with your packhorse, must climb step by step.

In the early nineteenth century a village was born as rows of houses clinging to rocks near the site of a quarry. Now, Tanygrisiau has a new purpose as a site for hydro-electric power generation. The system uses two lakes, one higher, the other lower. Power is generated as water from the top lake, Llyn Stwlan, drains to the artificially created Tanygrisiau reservoir. During off-peak periods at night, excess power from the national grid is used to pump water back to Stwlan for further generation.

In playing its new role, Tanygrisiau retains the feel of its traditional character: steep grades, terraces, the shop and post office, the railway station and the steam train with its re-assuring whistle. One could not mistake this place for somewhere else. Tanygrisiau is unique. Nearby is an area of special delight.

Coed Cymerau

To the south of Tanygrisiau is part of an ancient woodland, now a nature reserve. Coed Cymerau may be conveniently entered from the A496, which skirts it on the east, at GR 693440 and GR694431.

A mile southward along the A496 from Tanygrisiau, at GR493440, turn right over a footbridge spanning the Afon Goedal. The path meanders SW, turning eastward over the river to offer a grand waterfall view.

An exit point lies a few hundred yards eastward at GR694931. Continuing southward the path touches the A496 again at GR691421. Turning westward there is another footbridge spanning the river and, beyond it, the path winds up through deciduous woodland and a plantation to the Dduallt loop. See: **Walk in magnificent Snowdonia.**

Walk 24

Tanygrisiau — round the reservoir: 5.3km, 3.3ml.

From the station (0.0km) turn right past the Information Centre, fork left (0.2km), veer left at 0.7km to a footbridge and stile (0.8km) and on to stiles on either side of the railway line (0.9km) opposite the power station. Continue southward, past the occasional angler in pursuit of rainbow trout, to a footbridge at the southern end (2.1km).

Returning round the eastern side there is a fork (2.9km): one path leads westward round the shore, the other north-eastward. Both routes converge at a stepped wall stile (3.8km, taking the shore route). Continue E to a footbridge, on to the B4414 (4.6km) and turn left to the railway station.

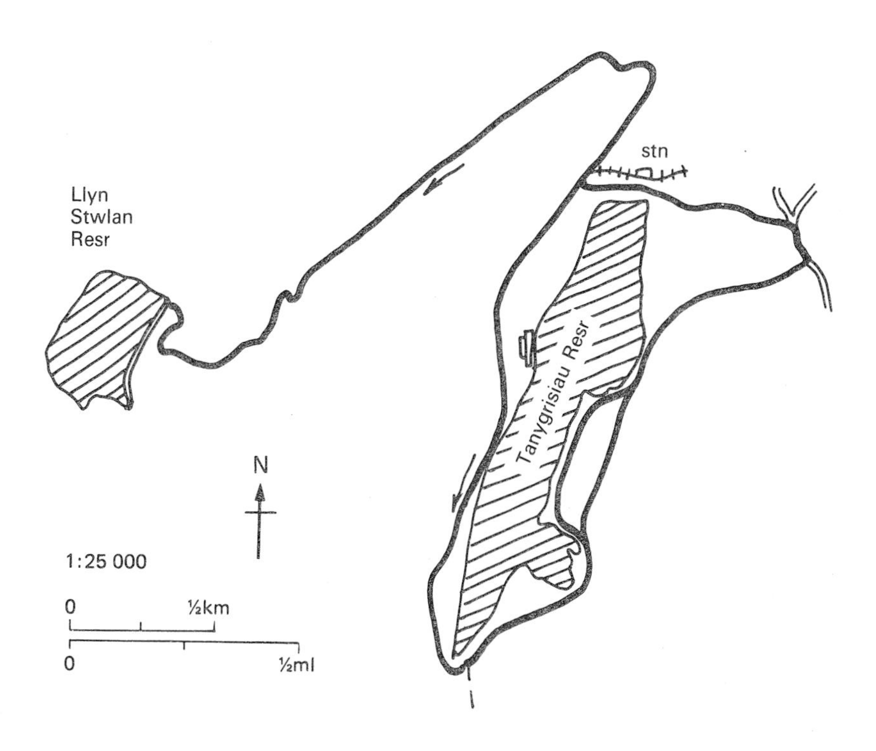

Walk 25

Tanygrisiau — Llyn Stwlan weir: 3km, 1.9ml.

Allow the environment to induce reflection. Gushing waterfalls draping massive boulders in silky, wispy white. From all directions, rugged ridges commanding attention. Capricious mists lying off, awaiting a propitious moment to descend.

The eyes keep returning from distant horizons to this Moelwyn massif, to mighty molars meticulously placed in monumental stone walls carrying tracks along which wealth was extracted from this place. The massive manual input expended in times before machinery makes the mind boggle. Such labour!

Those nameless labourers with no memorials should not be forgotten, remain unsaluted, unsung. Now, the only work done on the cliff faces is that of rock climbers practising their skills.

Walk along the top of the weir, down and around.

Where are the birds? Why do they shun this place? A mouthful of water from a gurgling stream feeding the reservoir leaves a dry peaty taste. One searches around the rocks as on a seashore when the tide is out. Where are the creatures burrowing, skurrying, freezing into immobility in defence? Rising water during the time of surplus power provides no haven for there is no life here.

The mist descends, doing its best to shroud the generating installation, trying to claim its own.

Walk 26

Tanygrisiau — Dduallt: 4.4km, 2¾ml.

Continue as for Walk 24 to the southern end of the reservoir (2.1km). Follow the track E then S to a gate and stile (2.5km), then soar above the level of the railway and plunge lower than it as an immaculately crafted stone causeway appears on the left. This was the route of the old Ffestiniog line before the construction of Tanygrisiau reservoir. We have the privilege of joining it (3.1km), stepping over the old sleepers still in place. Then appears the Dduallt station (3.6km) and that incredible phenomenon which will bear renewed contemplation — the Dduallt loop.

In the old days before the introduction of steam power this would have enabled two narrow-gauge trains to pass so that an unpowered down train kept gravitational momentum. What a fantastic device! Stand at the centre of the loop, where a direction dial has been erected on the mound reserved for viewing and picnicking, and see how magnificently it works.

From the southern end of the platform (3.7km) continue to Plas y Dduallt as in Walk 19.

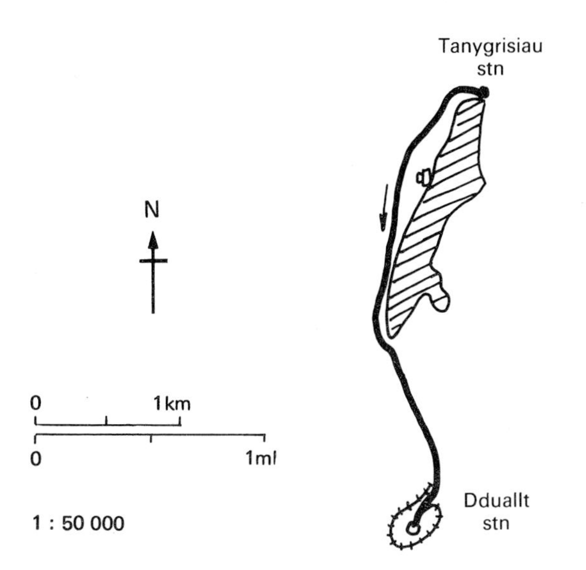

Walk 27

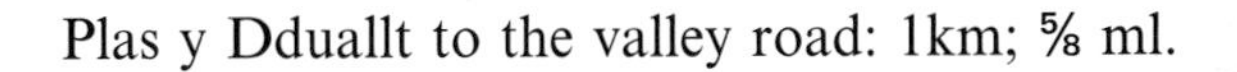

Plas y Dduallt to the valley road: 1km; ⅝ ml.

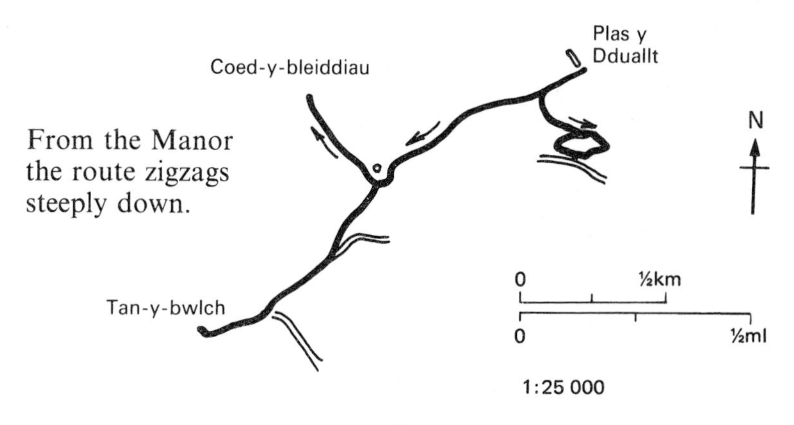

From the Manor the route zigzags steeply down.

Maentwrog village from the Afon Dwyryd early 20th century

Maentwrog village from the Gellilydan road early 20th century

Walk 28

Plas y Dduallt — Tan-y-bwlch 2km, 1¼ml.

From the Manor (0.0km) along the drive (250°) to a stile (0.4km), down to a footbridge spanning a silky stream issuing from a sparkling waterfall on the right. Continue W through the delightful Coedydd Maentwrog to a gate, turn right (W) past the cottage Bwthyn Bronturnor and over a footbridge (1.1km), fork left (SW) to a gate by the valley road and on to Tan-y-bwlch.

Walk 29

Plas y Dduallt — Coed-y-bleiddiau: 1.6km, 1ml.

As in Walk 28 to the footbridge (1.1km), fork right (W) up the hill, up and around a rocky outcrop, across the upper contours of a deep valley and NW to join the route of Walk 30 in *Coed-y-bleiddiau* — the wood of wolves, a name for this part of the forest that must be as old as Maentwrog across the valley.

Maentwrog

Place of *Legend*
Romance
Bardic Tradition
Aesthetic Harmony

In the fourth branch of the *Mabinogion* — the classic collection of Welsh folk legends — intrigue, deception and cunning thrive between the rulers of North and South Wales. A battle was fought, resulting in massive slaughter.

The northerners won: they were apparently better equipped with magic and enchantment, having had the experience of using these weapons with great craft to start the quarrel. The unfortunate overlord of the South — Pryderi by name — was slain and buried here at Maentwrog.

In the churchyard are three large yew trees reputably more than 1000 years old. Their lifespan reaches beyond another age. They shelter the graves of the Oakleys, creators of the village we see today.

William Griffith Oakley (1790–1835), son of a quarry master, was an aesthete who sought harmony between human construction and the environment. He personally supervised extraction of long blocks of stone, the shaping and dressing, then the careful fitting into walls with a minimum use of mortar. The Oakleys were fortunate in their choice of site — and so are we — for the high ground to the south and east, and low river plain to the north and west, preclude the type of twentieth-century development that would spoil this village.

The Oakley's home was at Plas Tan-y-bwlch, successor of earlier houses that represented the centre of an estate extending over a wide area of Eryri from Llanfrothen to Dolwyddelan. In the sixteenth century the incumbent squire was a descendant of the Welsh Prince Gruffydd ap Cynan, defender of Gwynedd against the intruder, King William II. It was a meeting place for bards where literary talents were fostered and generous hospitality provided. Then, in the eighteenth century, a daughter married William Oakley from Staffordshire and a new era began: into quarrying, land improvement and architecture. It was a fortunate development in that although the new arrivals were not mere seekers after wealth, upon acquiring it they had the talent to use it well. They sought to practise artistic excellence in their surroundings and they were promoters of education. These traditions continue at the Plas.

Walk 30

Plas y Dduallt — Tan-y-bwlch Railway Station:
3.2km, 2ml.

Fork right from the Manor (0.0km) to a stile (0.1km), on to a stream (0.3km) and into the Nature Reserve. The trail lies along an upper edge of the Vale close to the Ffestiniog railway line whose passengers are borne past fleetingly, leaving one to enjoy the expanse.

Beyond Coed y Bleiddiau cottage (1.0km), veer SW from the line, take a right fork (1.3km) and endure a transition from hardwood broadleaf to spruce pine.

Continue down to the B4410 (2.4km) and along the northern shore of beautiful Llyn Mair, named, so legend relates, because an unfortunate girl, Mair, submerged herself in response to unrequited love. Veer right (2.7km) into the centuries-old woodland known as Coed Llyn Mair. Cross the footbridge (3.0km) that spans a stream of pure crystal and continue to Tan-y-bwlch station.

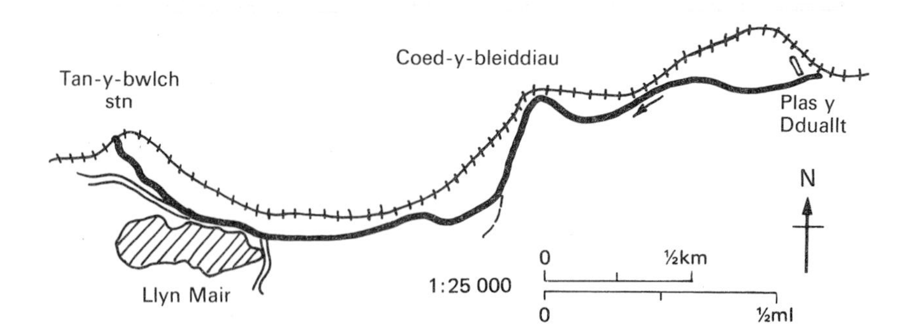

Study in symmetry on the Ffestiniog, late 19th century

Tan-y-bwlch *Confluence of Ancient Present Future*

Breathe the clean air — despite the railway and its steam locomotives and a main road lying alongside the shore of the lake — and note that on the bark of some trees are grey patches of lichens — evidence that the air really is unpolluted.

Looking southward from the station the woodland represents a fragment of how parts of high-rainfall Britain appeared after the Ice Age and before the age of industrialism.

Oak, the greatest British host for bird and insect life, has reproduced on this patch of ground, together with other natural hardwoods, for hundreds of years, providing examples for study of nature in pure form.

Walk 31

Tan-y-bwlch Railway Station — via Coedydd Maentwrog to east Penrhyndeudraeth: 4.3km, 2.7ml.

From the station (0.0km) walk SE along the path of the nature trail, established by the Nature Conservancy Council, leading to a stile (0.1km) and a footbridge by the B4410 (0.4km). Turn right (NW), past the turnoff to Tan-y-bwlch station (0.8km), under the railway bridge (0.9km) advertising its 1854 origin in the Boston Lodge Foundry, past the turnoff to Croesor and Beddgelert (1.0km). Five hundred metres along the road turn left (S) where sapling growths of oak, birch, rowan and blackberry briars seek to establish their birthright amongst the plantation.

Approaching a wall opening (1.9km) veer left (SE) with the wall on the right. Above Llyn Hafod-y-llyn veer to SW and hope to find a path if it has not been destroyed by planters. At a wall opening and stile (2.1km) take the fork SE and turn sharp right (W) then S and continue with pleasant hardwood and rhododendron on the right and encroaching pine on the left. There is an attractive view down to the SE end of the lake and a strangely incongruous sound of a steam locomotive puffing away a little more than a hundred yards somewhere beyond the wall of trees. One may divert down to the railway at 2.5km. A feature of this route is that, like the railway, it follows the contours.

There is a path-crossing at 2.8km, and 400m further on, a forestry road which has obliterated part of the path. Turn right (NW) along the road for 100m; turn left (S), by-passing a small lake on the left (3.3km). Continue on 250° for 300m, veer left from the wide path (still on 250°) down

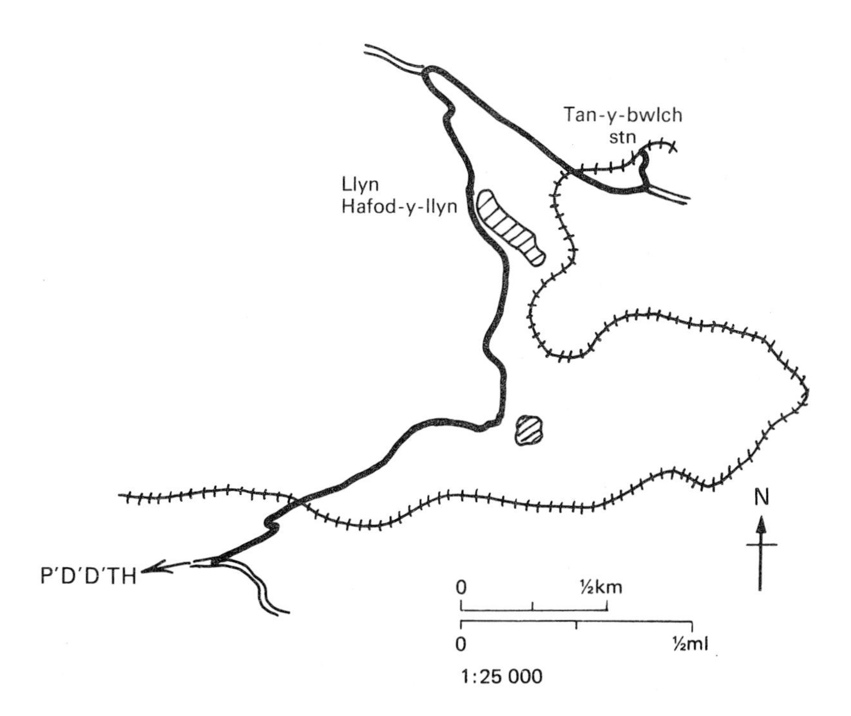

through the woods to a wall opening and, beyond it, stiles on either side of the railway line (3.7km). A steep path zigzags through the woods to a gate (4.2km) and the A487. Penrhyndeudraeth lies a little more than a mile south-westward.

Penrhyndeudraeth

Cockles
Independence
Radical
Tradition

On that neck of land which at one time was almost surrounded by sea — *penrhyn* means promontory or cape — there was a community known as "*cocosiaid y Penrhyn*" — the cocklers of Penrhyn. They were gatherers of cockles from the extensive stretches of beach sands to the north and south. To the north is *Traeth Mawr* — big beach — to the south *Traeth Bach* — small beach. *Penrhyndeudraeth*: cape between two beaches.

Y Traeth Mawr was referred to in the *Mabinogion*, and the two beaches in a book by Gerallt Gymro who travelled through Wales with Archbishop Baldwin in 1198.

Penrhyndeudraeth was identified under that name on a list of rates imposed by the conquering English king, Edward the First, in 1291.

Over the centuries, these isolated folk lived on their cape with two imperatives: subjection to the landlord and survival through self-sufficiency by working their plots and gathering a harvest from the sea. It was a background that — apparently — nurtured independent minds and a radical tradition.

A wind of change arrived in the eighteenth century with the ever-rising demand for slate, followed early in the following century by the building of the cob across the estuary. Linkage with the outside world brought change and opportunity. Penrhyndeudraeth developed downwards from the high ground, known as Cefn Coch, to the flat land below which had been drained by a local landowner — David Williams, Castelldeudraeth — later to become the local Member of Parliament.

Williams, although hardly a radical, was regarded by Penrhyn people as representative of their interests against those of absentee landlords who bribed, intimidated and punished in order to retain their hold on the parliamentary seat. Following the 1867 Reform Act, and consequent extension of the franchise, Williams of Penrhyndeudraeth was sent to parliament in the election of 1868.

Today, this community's roots show up like an irrepressible stream in its responses to the movements of our times. What is of concern to the country and the world is not ignored here behind the estuary of the two rivers. And the bards continue singing.

ix. Y ffin a welaf tros aber dwy afon
O benrhyn Llyn hyd ein traethell heno'n
Llwybr awennau lle bu Rhiannon
A'i hadar can hyd-ddo'n trydar cwynion
Alaeth yr hen gwerylon; — ffin liw rhudd,
A lliw'r hwyrddydd yw lloriau Iwerddon.

The boundary I see over the estuary of two rivers
From Llyn peninsula to our beach tonight
The path of lore trodden by Rhiannon
Along with her song birds chirping laments
Sorrows of old quarrels; — a crimson boundary
And the colour of eventide on the floors of Ireland.

Walk 32

Penrhyndeudraeth — Rhyd: 3km, 1.9ml.

From the Penrhyn Railway Station (0.0km), cross the road E, descend steps, turn left (N/NE). At 0.4km veer right, up steps and continue N under the railway line (0.5km). Turn right (N), right again (E), fork right, veer left (0.6km), continue on 060° to a gate (0.9km), a farmhouse (1.5km) and a gate (1.6km).

Alternatively, this walk may be commenced from a point one mile NE from Penrhyndeudraeth on the A487 (GR626401). A cart track bears 010° to the Ffestiniog Railway line (0.5km). Cross the line to the track bearing 060° from the village.

Walking this path one may hear a sharp bang and see a puff of smoke rise from behind a ridge to the south. This would be *bone fide* explosive makers testing their product. The explosive works was established last century in response to a growing demand from the quarries and has been in continuous production since.

Continue from the plantation boundary gate (2.0km), through gates at 2.5km and 2.7km to discover the pleasant hamlet of Rhyd.

Walk 33

Rhyd — Llanfrothen — Penrhyndeudraeth:
4.5km, 2.9ml

From Rhyd (0.0km) walk W to a stile (0.4km) at the side of the road and on the same bearing over three more stiles to a gate at the roadside (1.1km), turn left and, 100m along, left again (190°), veer to 240° and continue beside

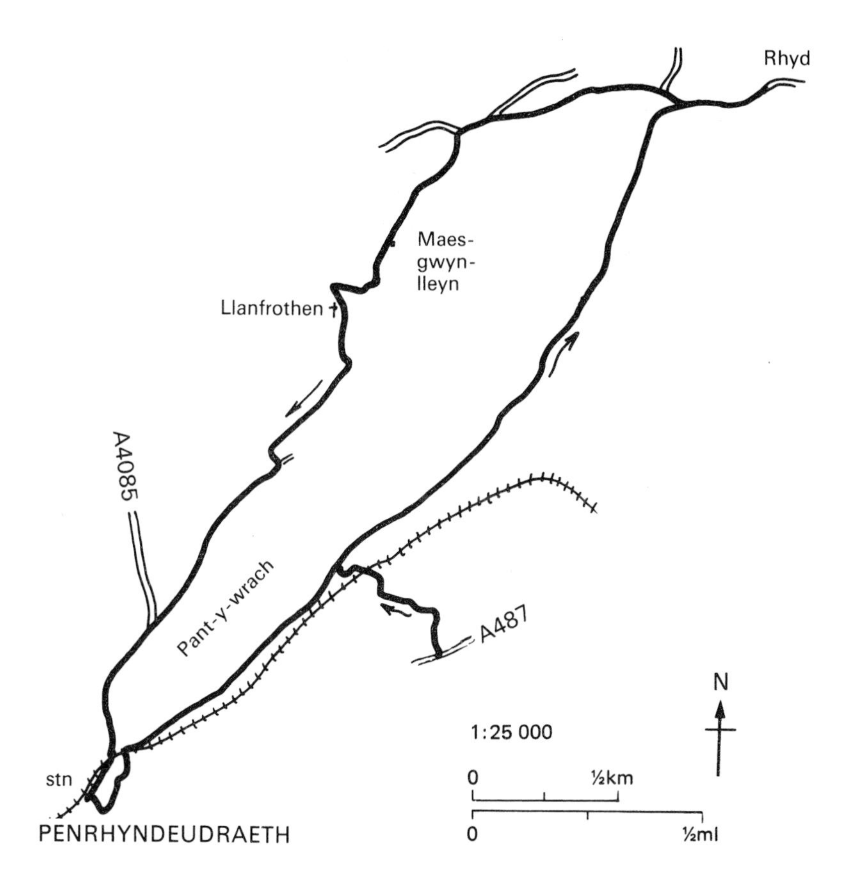
Rhyd
Maes-
gwyn-
lleyn
Llanfrothen
A4085
Pant-y-wrach
A487
stn
PENRHYNDEUDRAETH
1:25 000
N
0
½km
0
½ml

the right bank of the stream over a stile (1.5km) to another by the cottage Maes Gwyr Lleyn (1.7km). Continue down the drive to a gate (1.9km) and turn right to Llanfrothen. Should this village appear abandoned, giving an impression of ghosts in the churchyard, it might be as well to know that it is the centre of a wide area extending northward to Croesor and southward to Penrhyndeudraeth. Within that area there are cottage industries, not to mention a hotel soon to be discovered.

Turn left (2.1km) and bear S from the rear of the church over a footbridge, veering to 210° and SW. At 2.7km join a track originating at the rear of the Brynllydan Hotel, veer to SE and continue to a public road (3.0km). Turn right (S), then veer to SW through woodland which bears the name *Pant-y-wrach* (3.5km) — hollow of witches. Veer left (3.8km) along the A4058 across the Ffestiniog line (4.3km) to the Penrhyn Station.

Walk 34

Penrhyn Station — Ty-obry — Bwlch-glas — Penrhyn: 6.3km, 4ml.

From Penrhyn station (0.0km) cross the line, turn right (NE), veer left then right (0.2km), continue northward to a gate (0.3km) and a wall stile (0.4km). Further north 100m the path joins another beginning 100m east at the side of the B3310.

Continue W to a fence corner (0.6km), veer right through a gate to a farm drive, *Cae Merched* (0.8km) — field of women — W up the field to a stile (0.9km) and along the mound behind the farmhouse (1.0km). Veer to SW and continue through woodland to a plantation boundary stile (1.3km). This leads through the plantation to a farmhouse, Ty-obry, a distance of 300m. *Ty-obry*: the house below. Nearby is *Ty-fry*: the house above.

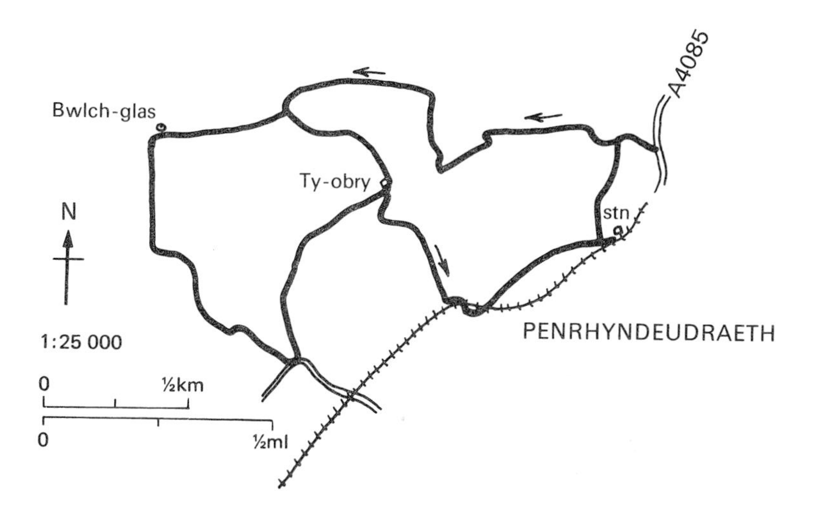

Alternatively from 1.3km, turn right along the outside of the plantation boundary to a stile (1.4km), northward down to a gate (1.7km), turn left (NW to W) and at 2.2km turn left again and follow a road winding south-eastward to Ty-obry (2.9km).

Alternatively at 2.2km, turn left then right over a cattle grid, passing the house Bwlch-glas (2.7km) on the right, turn left over a stile (2.8km) and continue S across the cob to a gate (3.2km) at the edge of the woods. Turn left (E) and continue S then SE through the woods to a road (3.9km). Turn left and left again (northward) past a caravan park on the left to a fork right (4.7km) onto a grass path and sharp right by the farmhouse, Ty-obry, up a broad grass slope bearing SW then S to a gate (5.0km), SE and S to a plantation boundary gate (5.3km).

Continue southward then E under the railway bridge (5.6km), turn left (NE) at 5.7km to a stile and veer right (E) alongside the railway, through a chapel's grounds and left to the Penrhyn station.

Walk 35

The estuary: 2.2km, 1.4ml.

From Penrhyndeudraeth's British Rail mainline station (0.0km), walk W for 100m, turn left (SW) across the railway line, SW past the house *Craig-y-don* — Rock of the wave — veer right (0.8km) then left to a critch-cratch (0.9km) and W across the flat of the estuary to a stile (1.2km) at the edge of the woods.

Turn right across the Cambrian railway line to a stile (1.3km), continue NE to a critch-cratch and on to the mainline station.

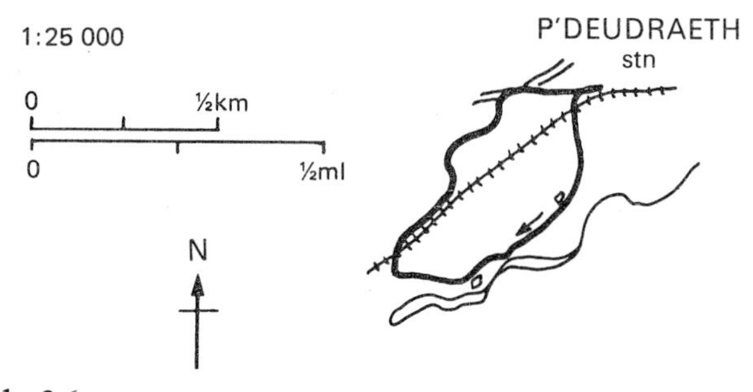

Walk 36

Minffordd — Portmeirion — Boston Lodge:
3km, 1.9ml.

From Minffordd PO (0.0km), walk 300m W along the A497, turn left (SW) into a lane and fork left at 0.8km to Plas Penrhyn (0.9km).

This Regency house was acquired by Bertrand Russell in 1955 and it was from here that Russell, in the late nineteen-fifties and early 'sixties, sent off messages to world heads of state concerning the preservation of international peace. It is thought that one of the reasons Russell was attracted to the area, and to Plas Penrhyn, was its association with the poet Shelley, who lived across the estuary at Tan-yr-allt above Tremadog — in 1812/13.

Continue 200m to the stables where paths diverge, and S to the boundary of the Portmeirion park (1.5km). Veer NW and W then SW (1.8km), and enjoy fine views of the estuary to Boston Lodge Railway Station.

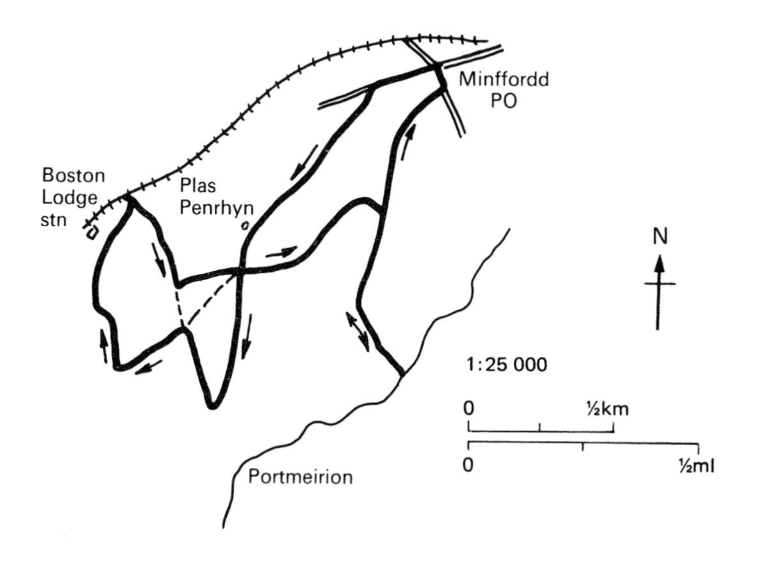

Walk 37

Boston Lodge — Minffordd: 2km, 1¼ml.

From the railway station (0.0km), veer left (SE) at 0.1 km and continue 300m to a gate, turn left (E) to a path junction at the stables (0.7km), on to a gate (1.0km) and NE through the woods to a road (1.3km). Cross the road to a junction (1.4km).

(The path southward past Cae-canol (200m), and then SE, is an attractive walk to the estuary shore, a distance of 700m).

Turn left from the junction (1.4km) and continue northeastward to Minffordd.

Cricieth

Sense
an Heroic
Age

This village is not in the Vale of Ffestiniog so why come here to begin an exploration of the Vale's seaward end? There are three reasons.

One is that on the top of the knoll behind which Cricieth shelters from the sea is a significant monument: the remains of a Welsh castle constructed by this country's greatest leader in the thirteenth century, Llywelyn Fawr, and later extended by the English following their conquest. Now a ruin it is an important relic of Wales's heroic age.

Another is that the farthest seaward expression of the Vale, Graig Ddu Traeth — Black Rock Sands — that magnificent expanse of beach which many people enjoy in summer, may be approached on foot from Cricieth via Graig Ddu itself and discovered in the manner of a revelation.

The third reason for coming to Cricieth is Moel Ednyfed, a hill behind the village which provides an opportunity to observe contrasts and proportions over a wide expanse of the area.

Cricieth Castle as it might have appeared at the end of the 13th century from a drawing by Alan Sorrell

Walk 38

Cricieth Castle — Moel Ednyfed: 2.2km, 1.4ml.

From the castle entrance (0.0km) bear N across the A497 along the B4411 to a turning right (1.2km) into a lane leading NE to Cefniwrch and a gate (1.3km), and on through several critch-cratches: along the edge of the field and a choice of routes to the summit.

The view seawards takes in most of Cardigan Bay, including the linear expanse of Black Rock and Harlech Sands, while the remainder of the full circle is a panorama of summits and ridges. In the immediate foreground Cricieth nestles like a faithful support platoon behind its castle.

Descend from the summit bearing 160° to a critch-cratch in the corner of the field, E along the field boundary to a gate and turn right (S) to Cricieth.

Walk 39

Cricieth Castle — Graig Ddu — Black Rock Sands:
3km, 1.9ml.

From the castle entrance (0.0km) walk E to the end of the esplanade (0.8km), and the gate by the railway crossing (0.9km), eastward along the path and across the line at 1.5km. At 1.8km there is a diversion NE which leads to the A497 via the farm Ystumllyn, offering a silhouette view of Moel-y-gest and its summit massif which awaits our ascent.

Continuing south-eastward, cross the line and bear 160° round the seaward side of Graig Ddu and up to the cliff top above the cave.

Graig Ddu and Black Rock Sands offer wonderful locations for contemplation of shore, sea and sky. Especially in calm conditions at the approach of evening when summer has departed.

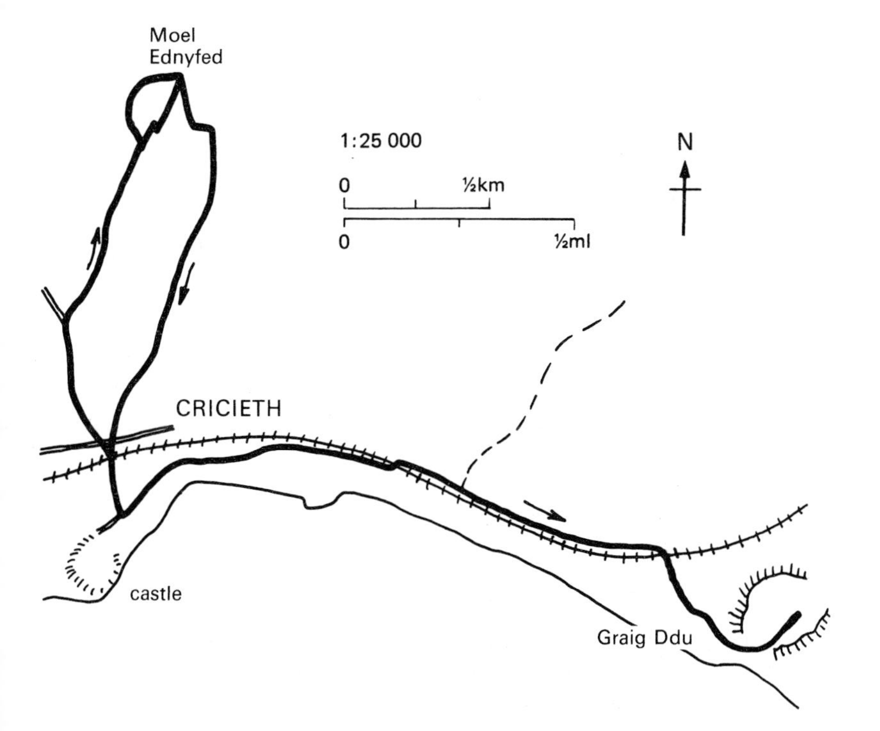
Moel
Ednyfed
1:25 000
0
½km
0
½ml
N
CRICIETH
castle
Graig Ddu

x. Tu allan, gwylan yn hwylio o’r golwg
heibio i’r Trwyn: neb ar y traeth:
yr hir ewyn yn derwyn wrth dorri:
y lliwiau yn nef y gorllewin —
aur mâl, tân a phorffor a melyn
a rhos yr hwyrnos — yn rhyw
bylu’n araf fel y suddai’r belen eirias
tu ôl i gaerau tawel y gorwel,
caerau o gymylau a’u myrdd
o dyrau yn dyrau o dan:
petrus sêr: ym mhellter y môr
hwyl wen ar fin diflannu
o’r hwyrnos a’r rhuddwawr arni.

Outside, a seagull sailing out of sight
beyond the cape: no-one on the beach:
the long foam brilliant when breaking:
the colours in the western sky —
wrought gold, fire and purple and yellow
and the rose of evening — somehow
dimming slowly as the molten ball sinks
behind quiet citadels of the horizon,
forts of clouds and their myriads
of towers being towers of fire:
uncertain stars: in distant sea
a white sail on brink of disappearing
from the evening taking its red hue.

In Porthmadog, amidst bustle in Stryd Fawr, one feels a need of height and space to consider this historic port in relation to the broad sweep of its surroundings. So, let the thrust be outward until a point is reached where one may take stock and contemplate.

Walk 40

Porthmadog — Tremadog: 3km, 1.9ml.

From the town side of the bridge that spans the Afon Glaslyn (0.0km), walk northward. At 0.6km there is a fork right (N/NE) which is on the return route if Walk 41 is followed. From the next junction (0.8km) the path lies along-

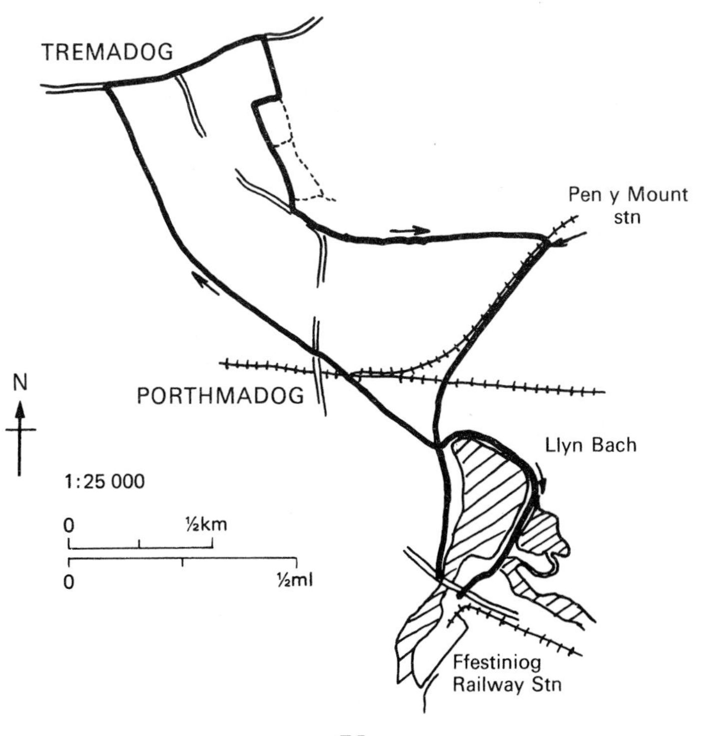

side Y Cyt — The Cut — which was designed to form a convenient transport link between two communities in the days when a canal was the most up-to-date transport mode. A piece of heritage awaiting suitable employment.

There is a stile (1.1km) adjacent to the British Rail Cambrian line and the Welsh Highland Light Railway Station, both lines meeting at this point. Cross the road (A487), fork right (340°) at 1.9km, continue to the main road (2.6km) and turn right to Tremadog.

Tremadog

Imagination
Perception
Resolution

The name is said to derive from Madog ap Owain Gwynedd who, according to tradition, sailed to the coast of America in the twelfth century. By coincidence, the name suggests the town's founder, William Alexander Madocks (1773–1828), Member of Parliament for Boston, Lincolnshire.

The concept of the Vale, as seen in human construction and operation today, is essentially that of Madocks more than any other individual. Madocks designed Tremadog. In the early nineteenth century he built the Cyt connecting Tremadog with what was to become the thriving port of Porthmadog. In 1807, he secured authority via a special Act of Parliament to build an embankment, now known as the Cob, across the estuary. About 5,000 acres of land were thereby reclaimed from the sea and a route was provided for the transport of slate by railway from the Ffestiniog quarries to the coast. This necessitated the building of port facilities which resulted in Porthmadog becoming part of a worldwide trading network.

However, Madocks' essential characteristic was that, like the Oakleys of Maentwrog, he sought to harmonise human

A vision of Porthmadog in 1810

construction with the environment. Look at Tremadog's spacious town square and well-designed buildings. The constructive imagination of the man inspired Percy Shelley who had taken the house, Tan-yr-allt, where he started to write his famous work Queen Mab. Shelley felt inspired by Madocks' philosophy and set about raising funds from local landowners in support of the embankment project. He also contributed from his own money despite personal indebtedness. Such was the poet's romantic idealism.

But still one must seek for a height in order to appreciate Madocks' grand concept.

Walk 41

Tremadog — Pen y Mount — Porthmadog: 4.7km, 3ml.

From Tremadog Square (0.0km) walk E for 400m and turn right (S) to a fork (0.6km). Southwards there are paths circulating these attractive woods. Fork right (W), then left (S) at 0.7km to the main road (1.2km), turn left, left again 100m further on and fork right (E). This lane leads to the present terminus, Pen y Mount (2.4km), of the Welsh Highland Light Railway which once connected Porthmadog to Beddgelert and Caernarfon, and is now in process of restoration.

From Pen y Mount station continue SW to the stile by the railway workshop (2.8km) — Gelert's Farm Works — and on to join the route of Walk 40 near the northern end of the tidal pool known as *Llyn Bach* — small lake. Turn left then fork right 100m further on, round the eastern side of Llyn Bach from where there is a good view of the old town and its protective mountain, Moel-y-gest, behind it. Cross the footbridge above the tidal sluice gates, and the twice daily inward and outward flow, to the Ffestinog Railway Station.

What kind of human story?

Technical feats there were a-plenty. The triumph of restoration following the official closure of the Ffestiniog Railway in 1946 is a story well told elsewhere. What made that triumph possible was the stirring of latent idealism by a vision of what might be. Not in the remote future but the here and now. The track lay to hand, some locomotives and rolling stock existed. Collective effort could make the vision real.

Any individual was welcome to become a volunteer, take part in a successful process, learn how to do various jobs, enjoy the comradeship of participation and see early achievement with a feeling of certainty that there would be much more to come.

That was the first phase of the project. The second was not less remarkable.

This was when the railway became a commercial operation, and the balance sheet might have rendered all that voluntary effort void. Idealism continued in a new guise: through the harmonious working together of paid staff with volunteers.

Proof can be felt in the general cheerfulness. It is infectious, whether from a guard's greeting as the train pulls into Tanygrisiau, a driver's wave out of a locomotive as it whistles through Coedydd Maentwrog, a sales assistant's smile at Tan-y-bwlch, or the pages of the quarterly magazine. The pervading impression is that these folk are enjoying themselves!

The place to share the enjoyment is on the train itself.

Porthmadog — Moel-y-gest summit: 7.5km, 4.7ml.

Leave Stryd Fawr — Porthmadog High Street — near Y Ganolfan (0.0km) and walk along and around dockland. But alas:

xi.

Aur hwyl ni throedia'r heli:
Ni ddaw llong dros ymchwydd lli,
Na llawen nwyf y rhwyfwr
Dewr ei daith hyd war y dŵr.

No gold sail graces the sea:
No ship rides the swelling tide,
Neither is there an oarsman
Setting out on the water.

It is a yacht basin now and beyond the haven is an array of mainly marine-associated industries and workshops, a busy place on a weekday morning. This labour-intensive scene suddenly gives way to sedate residential suburbia of discreetly spaced houses. When a pleasant bay appears — if the tide is in — we discover the seaside resort of Borth-y-gest (1.3km). Nothing discordant here; just an impression of pleasantness, sobriety, serenity.

On the farther side of the bay we pass the church (1.8km) onto a seafront path, forking right (2.1km) and, 100m further on, right (NW) to meet a broad path (2.4km).

Westward, the path continues amongst sand dune and seascape. But our destination is a mountain summit and, therefore, we must negotiate a spread of caravan parks. By a park corner veer right (N/NE), reaching a critch-cratch and the road (3.4km) near *Llyn Gareg Wen* — lake of the white stone. Here, we have a choice of route.

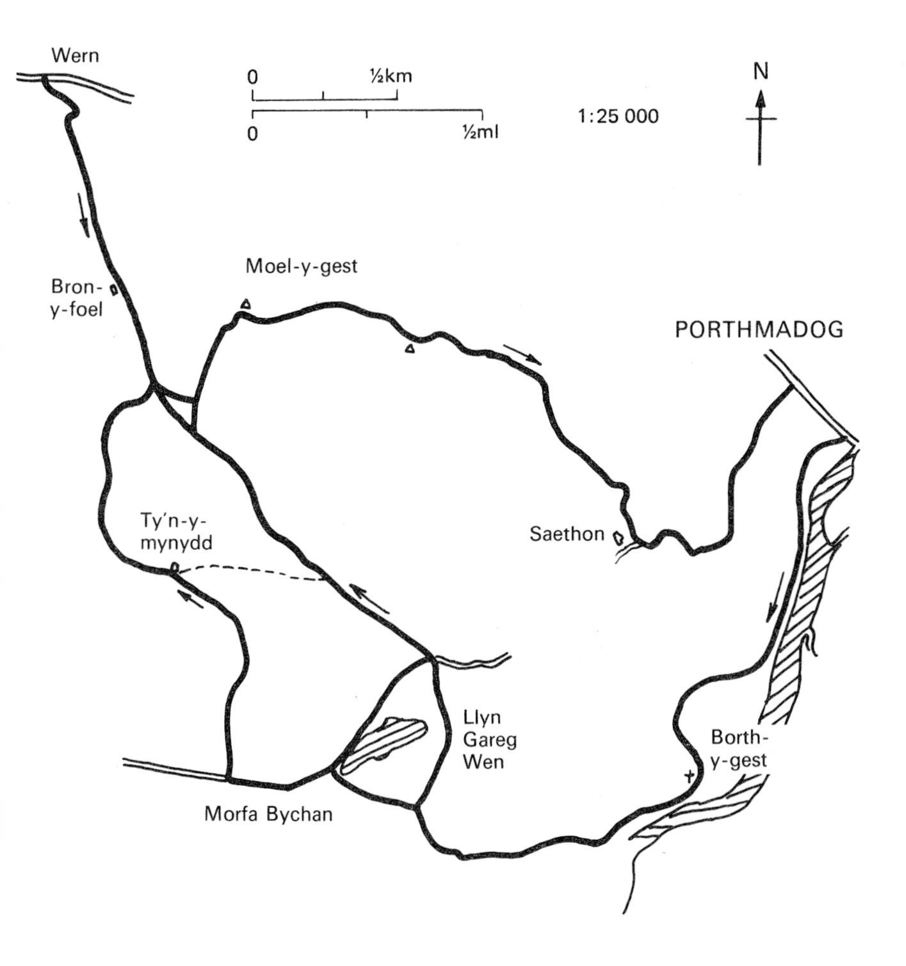
Wern
0
½km
0
½ml
1:25 000
N
Moel-y-gest
Bron-
y-foel
PORTHMADOG
Ty'n-y-
mynydd
Saethon
Llyn
Gareg
Wen
Borth-
y-gest
Morfa Bychan

Turning left, continue for about 800m, turn right and face the summit dead ahead north.

Alternatively from the park corner, continue to the SW tip of Llyn Gareg Wen, which appears wedged into the road fork, turn left and, about 300m along, turn right as above.

Fork left at 5.2m, veer right at 5.3km and right again at 5.5km. We now wind along and across the contours, ever upward.

One thing about this mountain is its truthfulness. It presents challengers with its true summit, honestly facing them in full frontal candour; not like some sly moels which proffer false summits while keeping the real one back!

And this moel is generous too. After passing the highest farm cottage, *Ty'n-y-mynydd* (6.1km) — house on the mountain — it offers its garden. If one is walking in the season of bloom, every colour of heather will be presented on this south-facing aspect : deep red, maroon, browns, fawns, purples, white.

Beyond a stile (6.7km), there is a gate 100m further on at the base of the summit massif.

Alternatively at the Morfa Bychan road (3.4km), cross to a wall stile and bear NW on a broad path to a gate (4.8km) beyond which the path forks. The left fork leads, in 700m, to the farm cottage, Ty'n-y-mynydd, and joins with the path described above about 100m beyond the cottage to the NW. The right fork leads NW to a gate (5.3km) and a wall stile (5.6km). Turn right (N) to the gate at the base of the summit massif.

This small mountain has yet another gift to bestow: an interesting and easy rock climb up its summit massif to the top.

xii

Tlws eu tw', liaws tawel, — gemau teg
 Gwmwd haul ac awel,
Crog glychau'r creigle uchel,
Fflur y main, ffiolau'r mêl.

Beautiful, quiet multitude, — fine gems
 Domain of sun and breeze,
Hanging bells of the high rock,
Slender flowers, phials of honey.

Walk 43

Wern — Moel-y-gest summit: 2km, 1¼ml.

From a point on the A497 near Wern (0.0km) walk up the farm track, forking left at 0.9km onto a green path rising from the farmhouse Bron-y-foel, then to a gate (1.4km), a wall opening (1.5m), E to the gate where these routes converge and up the rocks to the summit.

From the Moel-y-gest summit, *Mynydd Ednyfed* behind Cricieth is a mere pimple on the landscape. *Morpha Bychan* is a flat square sandwich on the immense sweep of Cardigan Bay. *Borth-y-gest* is the tiny fishing village it once was. This is a place to review one's sense of proportion. Opportunities for doing so are unusual because Moel-y-gest has two summits, western and eastern, with a connecting ridge which provides excellent viewing.

Walk 44

Moel-y-gest west summit — east summit: 1.2km, ¾ml.

Moving east from the west summit (0.0km), this moel reveals itself as just the right size for its locality, not being so high that it overpowers its surroundings while providing suitable distance for detached intimacy. Down there at the foot of Craig y Castell, below the house, Tan-yr-allt, where Shelley lived, is William Madocks' Tremadog. Madocks was one of those few individuals whose work endures. He planned Tremadog as a model community and from this height one can see a broad square and wide streets with the Cyt forming a logical transport link to the seaboard, and, ultimately, to the world. Fortunately, the modern development southwards blends with Madocks' design — almost as if the planner had himself foreseen the kind of challenges with which his creation would have to contend.

Porthmadog — a world port

Imagine a single mind working to an overall concept of two communities, linked but playing separate roles, set harmoniously in a broad expanse of hinterland. It was a response to a basic commercial stimulus that is now past.

A bard sings of what is everlasting.

xiii.

Mae'r llanw'n dal i ddyfod,
  A chilio'n ol yn slei,
Gan adael sawrau gwymon
  I loetran lond y cei;
A chyffry'r cychod bach am dro
O'u gogwydd diog ar y gro.

The tide rises as ever,
  And withdraws slyly,
Leaving odours of seaweed
  Loitering over the quay;
And rousing small boats to life
From slumbers on the gravel.

He laments for the past.

Ac nid oes neb yn tremio'n
  Ddisgwylgar dros y bar,
Fe ddarfu'r son am 'Frisco,
  Brisbane a Zanzibar;
'Does neb yn malio mwy am sgorn
Y moryn hwnnw gylch yr Horn.

And there is no-one gazing
  Watchfully over the bar,
Vanished the talk of 'Frisco,
  Brisbane and Zanzibar;
No-one feels moved by the scorn
Of that sea about the Horn.

Loading Ffestiniog slate onto a schooner at Grave's Wharf, Porthmadog

He sings joyously for the present.

Mae rheiliau'r Cob yn tasgu
Dan dywyn haul y nawn,
A Prins yn tynnu'n galed
A'r holl gerbydau'n llawn;
Mae'r hen dren bach yn talu'n dda
A'i siwrnai'n 'mestyn Ha' 'rol Ha'.

The rails of the Cob shimmer
Beneath the afternoon sun,
And Prince is pulling strongly
With all his carriages full;
The *tren bach* is paying well
Its line advancing each year.

With the line fully restored and renowned worldwide, this old port has acquired new significance.

A view of Porthmadog from Moel-y-gest's east summit includes a rectangular patch of the built environment which has three railways — surely, an incomparable distinction. The smallest, with stout heart and mighty ambition, is apt to make the most noise, possibly because its engine is continually changing ends to serve its very short stretch of line from Porthmadog to Pen y Mount, a distance of barely a mile. But the future stretches away into the distance along the route northward across Traeth Mawr and on to Beddgelert which was settled way back in the mists of time, more than a thousand years ago, by monks looking for peace and quiet. While cherishing tranquillity and seclusion from the secular world they created a priory which endured for many centuries but had disappeared long before the highland railway arrived on the scene.

Walk 45

East Summit of Moel-y-gest — Porthmadog: 4km, 2½ml.

Reluctantly, one takes leave of this place, descending into a garden of heathers, if here in the season of bloom; tacking across a scree of boulders, down to a path (1.9km), then to a wall stile (2.0km), a fence stile (2.3km), past Saethon (3.0km) to Stryd Fawr.

Walk 46

Porthmadog — Beddgelert: 15km, 9.4ml.

From the Welsh Highland Railway Station (0.0km) walk SE for 300m, turn left (NE) over the bridge, cross the British Rail line (0.5km), continue past Gelert's Farm Works of the W.H.L.R. on the left and follow the path to Pen y Mount Station.

Follow the course of the old railway along its embankment, passing over stiles every two to three hundred metres to a stile at 2.9km. Veer left to the next stile (3.1km), then to a critch-cratch (3.2km) near the course of a winding stream, turn right to a gate and left along the railway embankment. Beyond a stile at 3.8km is the Afon Glaslyn (4.5km) — Pont Croesor, an objective of restoration for the railway company in its long haul up the valley. Here a broad river must be bridged, a river which, when it overflows its banks flooding adjacent flat fields, creates an impression of how this area must have appeared when Traeth Mawr was under the sea.

Along a stretch of road adjacent to the old railway track is a stile at 5.7km. Continue, veering from 070° to 040°.

At 7.2km veer left to 310°; at 7.7km there is a long curve to 340° leading to an undecked bridge (8.0km); 200m further on cross the bridge spanning the Afon Dylif, a tributary of the Glaslyn. The next bridge (8.9km), across the

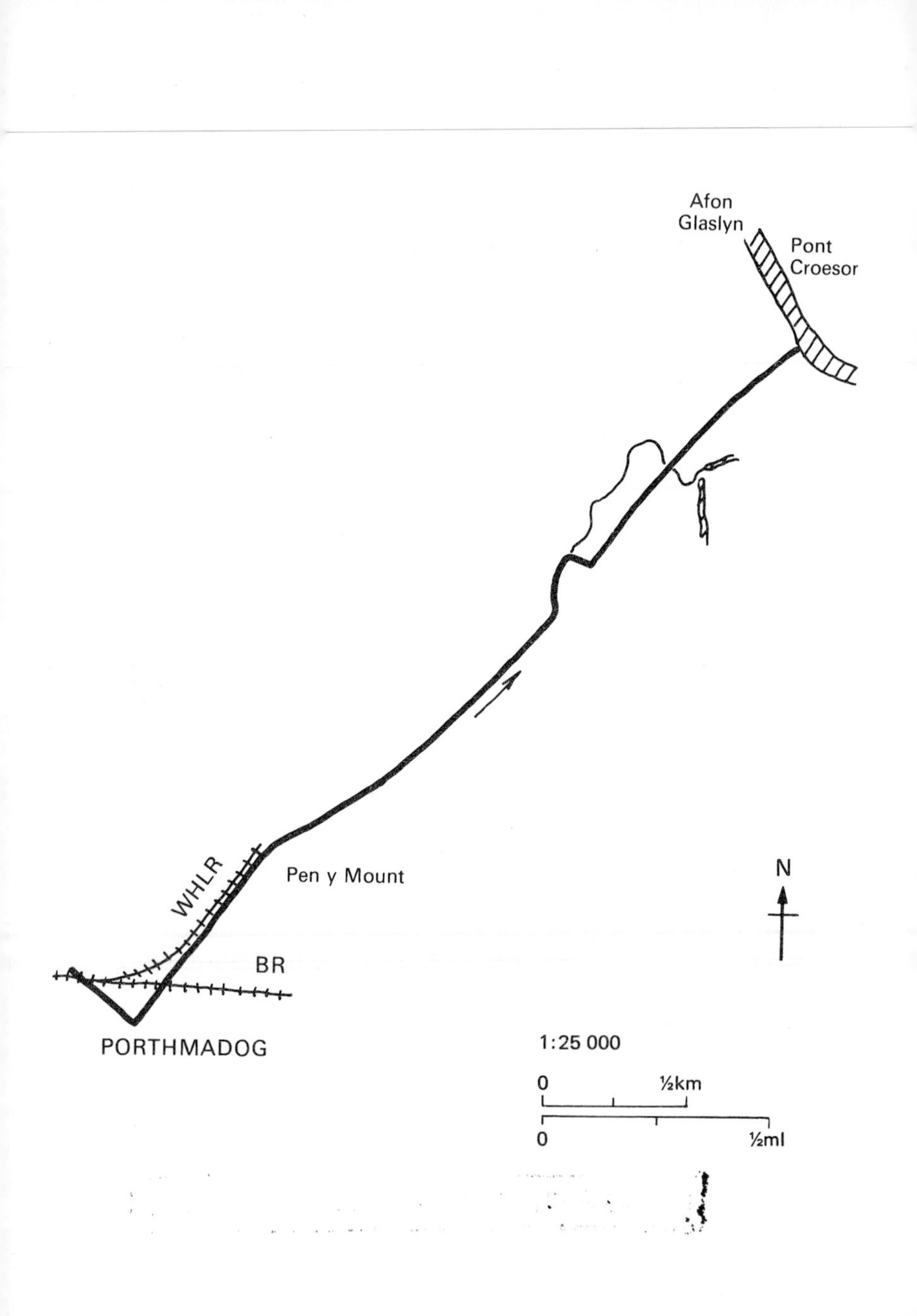
Afon
Glaslyn
Pont
Croesor
WHLR
Pen y Mount
BR
PORTHMADOG
N
1:25 000
0
½km
0
½ml

Afon Nanmor, another tributary of the Glaslyn, has been decked and gated as a footbridge. The track veers round hillocks (N) to a stile (9.2km); then, on 340°, round wooded low cliffs to 025° and on to a stile near the Afon Glaslyn (10.8km); then along an embankment to an undecked bridge across the A4085 (11.3km). Continue through a cutting, over an embankment on a short curve to 325°, through another cutting to 345° and a straight stretch crossing the Nantmor Road (11.9km); then through cuttings, across a high embankment and into a tunnel (12.2km) with no light at the end of it!

Proceeding hopefully, the way ahead lightens round the tunnel bend. After emerging (12.6km), enter two short stretches of tunnel and then, if the season is May or early June, discover a display of wild rhododendrons on the west-facing hillsides. Copper is thought to be the nutrient that causes the brilliant blooming. The mineral was mined here by a German company before the First World War. Some of the old Sygun copper mines have been interestingly restored.

Cross the Glaslyn via another railway bridge (13.7km), continue under a road bridge carrying the A498, through a long-curved cutting and along the base of the hillsides to our destination near the rear of the Royal Goat Hotel, Beddgelert.

So, we have emerged from the Vale of Ffestiniog into another vale — that of the Aber Glaslyn.

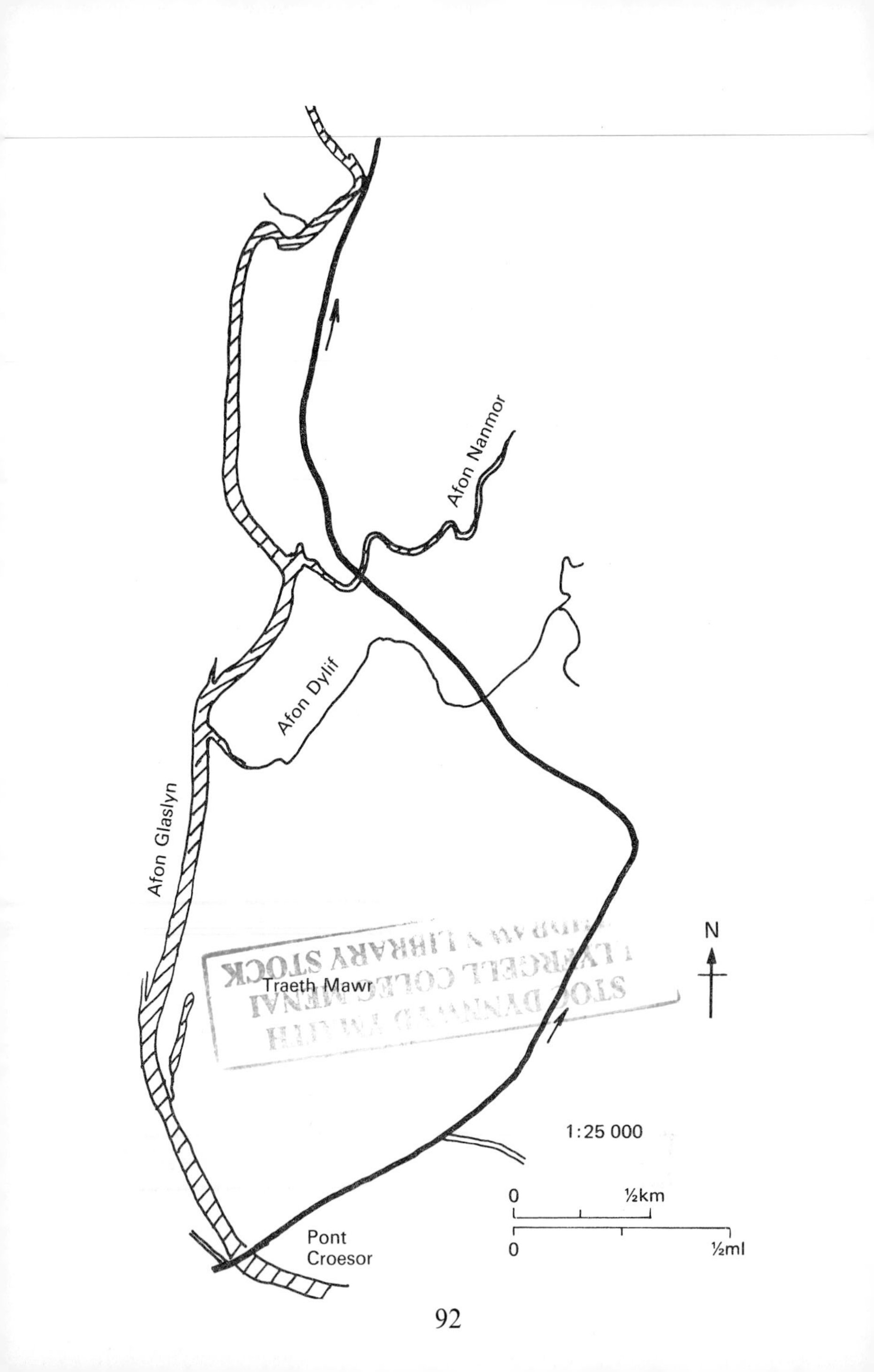
Afon Nanmor
Afon Dylif
Afon Glaslyn
Traeth Mawr
N
1:25 000
0
½km
0
½ml
Pont
Croesor

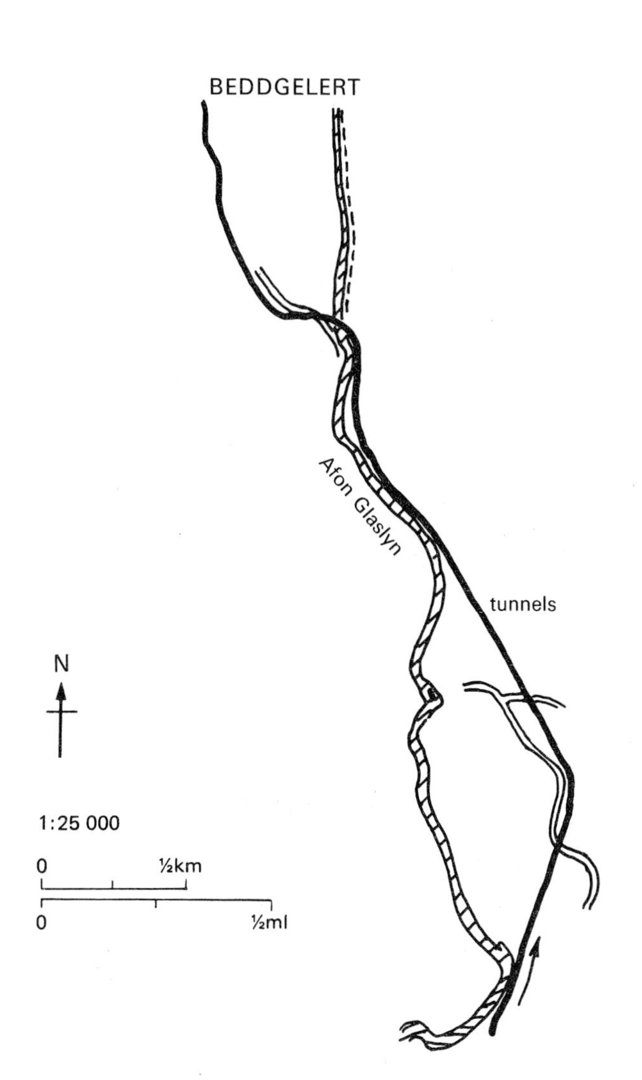
BEDDGELERT
Afon Glaslyn
tunnels
N
1:25 000
0
½km
0
½ml

Bards' Roll

i. **Y Moelwyn** Hedd Wyn (1887-1917)

ii. **Y Gorwel** David Emrys James
The Oxford Book of Welsh Verse O.U.P. 1983

iii. **Cerdd yr Hen Chwarelwr** William John Gruffydd
(1881–1954) The Oxford Book of Welsh Verse

iv. **Y Moelwyn Mawr a'r Moelwyn Bach** William Jones
(1896–1961) The Oxford Book of Welsh Verse

v. **Afon** Ieuan Jones, Dyffryn Ardudwy

vi. **Yr Hen Felin** Monallt Llyfrfa'r M.C.
Caernarfon 1969

vii. **Y Ffin** J Rowland Hughes
Can Deu Ddwy Gwasg Gee Dinbych 1982

viii. **Y Coedwigwr** Monallt Llyfrfa'r M.C.

ix. **Gorwel** Ieuan Jones, Dyffryn Ardudwy

x. **Hwyrnos** J Rowland Hughes Can Neu Ddwy

xi. **Y Ffin** J Rowland Hughes Can Neu Ddwy

xii. **Blodau'r Grug** Eifion Wyn
The Oxford Book of Welsh Verse

xiii. **Porthmadog** Ieuan Jones Dyffryn Ardudwy

Bibliography

Winson, J., *The Little Wonder*, Ffestiniog Railway Company and Michael Joseph, 1975

Nash-Williams, V.E., Jarrett, M.G., *The Roman Frontier in Wales*, University of Wales Press, Cardiff 1969

Jones, A., *A History Of Gruffydd ap Cynan*, University of Manchester Press, 1910

Roberts, J.H., *Cerddi Monallt*, Llyfrfa'r M.C., Caernarfon 1969

Rowland Hughes, J., *Can Neu Ddwy*, Gwasg Gee, Dinbych 1982

Parry, T., (editor), *The Oxford Book Of Welsh Verse*, O.U.P. 1983

Jones, J; Jones, T; (translators), *The Mabinogion*, Dent 1989

Jones, I., *Poems*

Ordnance Survey publications

Acknowledgements

For permission to reproduce archive material in possession of:

THE NATIONAL LIBRARY OF WALES
(illustration 7)

GWYNEDD ARCHIVES SERVICE
(illustrations 1, 2, 3, 4, 5, 6, 8, 12, 13, 15)

WELSH FOLK MUSEUM, ST FAGAN'S
(Illustrations 9, 10)

NATIONAL MUSEUM OF WALES/
WELSH INDUSTRIAL AND MARITIME MUSEUM
(illustrations 11, 14)

For information:

Evan Vaughan Jones, Meiriondy, Penrhyndeudraeth.

Geraint Lloyd Jones, Llwyn Hudol, Penrhyndeudraeth.

Albert Humphreys, Penrhyndeudraeth.

R.D. Morgan, conductor of The Royal Oakley Band, Blaenau Ffestiniog.

R.D. Jones, publicity officer, Côr Meibion y Moelwyn, Blaenau Ffestiniog.

Arthur L. Davies, secretary, Côr Meibion y Brythoniaid, Blaenau Ffestiniog.